CITIZEN'S GUIDE TO CALIFORNIA WINE COUNTRY
NAPA AND SONOMA

By
Heidi Butzine

**Wineopolis
Citizen's Guide to California Wine Country
Napa and Sonoma**

Copyright © 2010 Heidi Butzine
All rights reserved.

Published by Wineopolis Press
legal@wineopolispress.com
http://www.wineopolispress.com
409 N Pacific Coast Highway, Suite 260, Redondo Beach, CA 90277

ISBN 978-0-9826922-0-2

Printed in the United States of America.

NOTICES:

All rights reserved. No part of this publication may be reproduced or transmitted in any form or by any means, electronic or mechanical, including photocopying, recording or by any information storage and retrieval system without express written permission from the publisher.

Every attempt has been made to ensure accuracy of the information contained in this publication at the time of publishing, however, publishers cannot accept responsibility for any errors it may contain. Before traveling, we recommend that you confirm rates and prices with the establishments directly.

Contents

Chapter I.	Introduction to the Northern California Wine Country 1	
	A Little Taste of Napa & Sonoma 1	
	History Highlights 3	
	Tips for Making Your Itinerary 4	
	When to Go 6	
Chapter II.	**A Brief Study on Wine Tasting** 9	
	How to Taste a Wine 10	
	Pairing Wine with Food 12	
	Best Flavors of the Region 13	
	Don't Go Home Empty Handed! (Bringing Wine Back) 14	
Chapter III.	Experiencing Napa 17	
	All About Napa 17	
	Wine:	Napa Wineries 22
	Dine:	Napa Restaurants 52
	See:	Activities not to be missed 64
	Stay:	Where to stay 76
Chapter IV.	Experiencing Sonoma 93	
	All About Sonoma 93	
	Wine:	Sonoma Wineries 99
	Dine:	Sonoma Restaurants 128
	See:	Activities not to be missed 140
	Stay:	Where to stay 152
Chapter V.	Getting Around and Other Important Stuff 167	
	Travel by Air, Train and Auto 167	
	Local Transportation Options 172	
	Tasting Wine…Responsibly 176	
Chapter VI.	Some Wine Terms You Need to Know 177	
	Index 181	

Welcome to Wineopolis

Rediscover the Wisdom of the Ages

Congratulations! You are an honorary citizen of the society of *Wineopolis*. This is your passport to exploration and discovery of some of the most beautiful wine regions in the world.

Wine has long been cherished as a gift to be shared and enjoyed by all. The ancient Greeks would honor their spirit divinity Dionysus with days-long festivals overflowing with wine and fine food and the bonding of community.

We, the citizens of Wineopolis, are from all regions and backgrounds, and have come together to share the enjoyment of life through wine and food – much like the Dionysus festivals of old. We are building an interactive online community where everyone can take part in learning about wine and sharing their experiences to help enrich others. We are all wine novices and wine experts.

No longer is the world of wine intimidating or enjoyed by only the elite. It's time to take our love of wine back and relish in the divinity inherent in each glorious sip. Thanks to the emergence of the virtual world, Wineopolis is ready to take you on a journey through the senses as only a great glass of wine can deliver.

As a citizen of Wineopolis, not only will you develop your own wine tasting expertise, you will enhance your knowledge of wine, its place in our history as well as in our modern society – giving you some bragging rights amongst wine lovers. By taking an active part in the community and sharing your wine tasting experiences, food finds, your travel logs, you are spreading knowledge. We are unique citizens who have created a community to bring the art of wine back to the masses, one glass at a time.

We get what we give, and that is true for the citizens of Wineopolis who honor life through the sharing and enjoyment of wine and food with others.

But perhaps the best benefit to joining Wineopolis is that you are becoming a member of a close-knit community where you can find new like-minded friends.

So talk with us, read some inspiring stories, share your own adventures, and then go out into the world ready to find that undiscovered vintage. Re-learn what our ancestors knew and lived – wine is not only an experience; it's a way of life.

About the Author

It was her first trip to the Tuscan wine region that inspired Heidi to begin writing about her life-long passion for food, wine and travel. Appreciating wine and food - not as a commodity, but as a way of life - was something that Heidi wanted others to experience too. This inspiration soon became a goal for Heidi to establish Wineopolis; a community of wine lovers, where everyone can take part in learning about wine and sharing their experiences to help enrich each other.

Heidi's journey continues to build upon her travels to wine regions across the globe, gathering first-hand knowledge about regional wine and food and how they influence life, culture and history. As a wine aficionado, Heidi has studied food and wine with local experts throughout Italy and France as well as at the Culinary Institute of America in the heart of Napa Valley.

Following a decade-long career as a founding partner of a consulting firm, Heidi is now applying her business expertise towards launching and growing new ventures devoted to wine lovers. Since 2006, Heidi has been writing wine-related articles which are now featured at her company blog. Although writing started as a hobby to convey her passion, it has now become the foundation for her latest business ventures Wineopolis. com, Wineopolis Press and Bliss Discovery Group, Inc. Heidi is the author of the *Bartender's Association Internationale's Certified Wine Expert Training Program* for and the *Wineopolis Travel Guidebook* series.

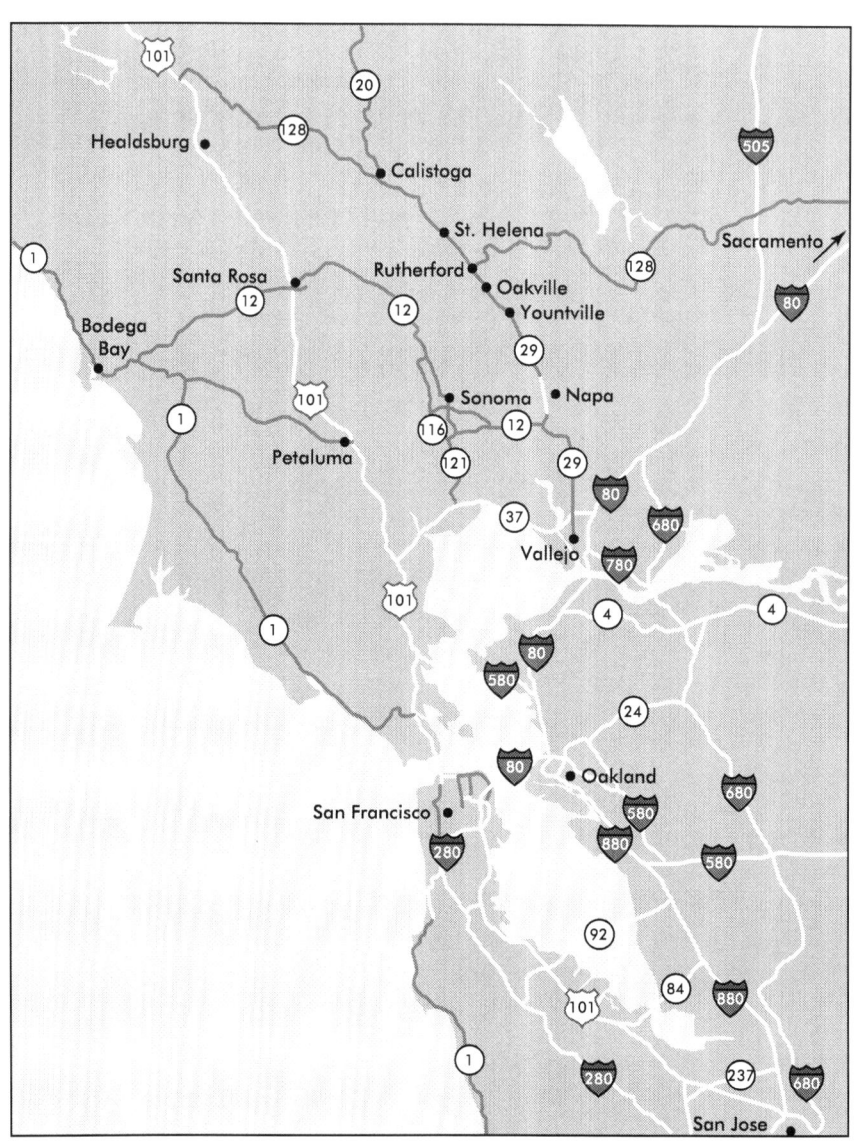

I. Introduction to the Northern California Wine Country

Get prepared to travel to one of the most beautiful, dazzling and exciting wine regions in the country, heck we'll even say the world. Northern California is home to some of the most talked about wineries, for good reason. The climate is perfect, the people are swell, and the wines are just plain awesome. The regions we'll be talking about in depth are the counties of Napa and Sonoma. They both encompass quite a large area of some of the most beautiful land to ever grow a grape. We'll bet you've even heard the names of these wines a time or two or read it on a bottle. But now it's time to really get to know the best that these two regions have to offer, because they offer quite a bit. Whether you're planning your first trip to the region or you've been here before and are looking to expand your experience, this is the book for you. We've been here, we've seen it all, and we're ready to share the best of the best.

So sit back, relax, and start some California Wine Dreamin'...

A Little Taste of Napa and Sonoma

Napa and Sonoma are two of the most prestigious Wine Country regions loved by wine experts and novices alike. You can spend a lifetime here and not get enough of the hundreds, yes *hundreds* of wineries spread across the region. But don't despair. We're here to help point out what your must dos are.

Napa and Sonoma are located about an hour north of San Francisco in the northern part of California. Napa sits inland in a vast stretch of rolling hills and farmland, while Sonoma borders the Pacific Ocean then stretches inland across a gentle mountain range. Both areas are slightly different in geographic makeup and this shows in the nature of the wines produced in each appellation within Wine Country. We'll start with Napa.

Napa

Napa, commonly referred to as Napa Valley, is the more rural of the two regions, though it has risen in popularity, thus also in population, over the last several years. Its meteoric rise in popularity is probably thanks to the many celebrity clientele who have decided to move here and take on the wine business. The area boasts residents such as Robert Redford, Robin Williams, Mario Andretti, Danielle Steele, and Francis Ford Coppola (who has his own winery, by the way). However, it still remains the least populated county in the North Bay, thus giving the region a very quaint country feel.

Napa consists of a narrow stretch of land starting with the town of Napa. The town only has a population of about 75,000 people, yet it is the most populated town in the whole county. See what we mean by rural? Napa has a main drag called Soscol Avenue which houses all sorts of shops, restaurants and wine-related souvenirs. But the true beauty of the region lies in the surrounding landscape. It is estimated that Napa County has more than 300 wineries! You could spend a lifetime here, it seems, and not hit them all. But don't worry, we're going to make sure you know the highlights.

Sonoma

If Napa is considered "country", then Sonoma County is more of a "city" cousin. Sonoma is not only more populated than Napa, it is dotted with larger towns along Highway 101 as it stretches north from San Francisco up through Cloverdale. Outside the 101 corridor, however, is mainly sprawling farmland which grows many fruits and vegetables, as well as grapes. The biggest city on this drag is Santa Rosa located in the middle part of the region. Santa Rosa is split across the highway, with rows of antique shops, souvenir shops, eateries and coffeehouses to be found in either direction. The town of Sonoma is further south and is much less populated and more historic in makeup, housing the Mission San Francisco de Solano as well as many well known wineries.

Another big draw to Sonoma County is that it borders the Pacific Ocean on the west. Visitors can drive up historic Highway 1 which

Share your experiences online at wineopolis.com

hugs the coastline and offers some of the most stunning ocean views along the west coast. Most famous along this route is Bodega Bay, a large fishing enclave that boasts stunning cliff vistas as well as sandy beaches.

Both Napa and Sonoma are the home to some of the most prestigious wineries in the world. But before we start salivating, let's discuss the regions where the grapes are grown, called appellations.

Appellations

In regards to wine, an *appellation* is a geographic area where a grape is grown. This is what identifies a wine and will tell you exactly where the grapes come from. It's easy to determine, as wine bottles will list the appellation on the label, if they have one. The standard is that for a wine to list an appellation it must have at least 85% of the grapes that are used in that wine to come from that geographic area. Appellations in the U.S. have been designated by the initials AVA, which stands for American Viticultural Area. A list of the appellations to be found in Napa and Sonoma are included in this book, so you can determine which ones you want to visit or look for in your local wine shop.

Once you start tasting wines from different regions, you will be able to determine which regions have the best grapes. For instance, a Chardonnay from one appellation might be consistently better than other Chardonnays. An appellation can be very prestigious. If a wine wants to boast that it's from a Napa Valley appellation, they must get the majority of their grapes from there or else they cannot claim it. Wines from all regions that cannot claim an appellation must use a more generic reference area, such as being a California wine.

Napa and Sonoma have many appellations and when we list specific wineries, we will also be listing the appellation that they belong to. Now, let's take a moment to learn a little history about the region.

History Highlights

California has an exciting history, especially in the northern regions. In 1848 a carpenter stumbled upon a golden nugget while working in the Sierra Foothills. What ensued has come to be known as the Gold Rush of 1849. Folks from all over the United States and beyond flocked to the region to dig for their fortunes in a brand new state acquired only years before from Mexico.

Before the rush, however, the northern region was the home to many indigenous Indians. Tribes such as the Miwok, Mayacama and Pomo spread across the landscape. The mild climate made for fruitful farming. The region north of San Francisco was mostly wilderness and largely unsettled except for a miner or two until the Gold Rush changed

Share your experiences online at wineopolis.com

this dramatically. As the population boomed, wilderness made way for civilization. As cities cropped up, so did farmland.

We're not real sure exactly when grapes began to be grown. In Napa, two early settlers to the region both grew grapes: frontiersman George Yount and English surgeon Dr. Edward Bale. Though not necessarily for the making of wine for commercial purposes, both settlers farmed the land, erected mills and recognized the climate was perfect for growing vines. It wasn't until some German settlers made their way to the area that grapes were cultivated into wines. Recognized names such as Charles Krug, Jacob and Frederick Beringer and Gottlieb Groezinger are still honored in the region for their early cultivation.

However, the man credited with first recognizing the potential for grape cultivation in the region is Count Agoston Haraszthy. He is considered the father of viticulture (which means the cultivation of grapes and grapevines). Like many others, the Count arrived in northern California during the rush. However, sometime in the 1850s he realized his fortune was in the soil surrounding the area of Sonoma. Convinced it was perfect for the growing of vines, he traveled back to Europe, gathered as many varietals of grapes as he could muster and returned with almost 300 different cuttings to plant in the region. What ensued was something of a "Grape Rush" and the region had found a new claim to fame.

By the 1870s, wine was becoming business in the region and even though there were a few setbacks along the way (most notably drought and prohibition), viticulture has never been more popular than it is today.

Now that you have a little history and lay of the land, let's get to making plans to visit.

Tips for Making Your Itinerary

There are a few things you need to know before you go, especially if you're new to the practice of wine tasting. It is estimated that Napa and Sonoma both have upwards of four million visitors per year. That's a lot for a relatively small area and wine tasting rooms can get crowded pretty quick depending on when you go. So the idea of just "showing up" is not advised. Just like most other vacations you take, planning is essential to making the most of your visit.

Here are some things you will want to keep in mind when setting your itinerary:

1. *Have a route in mind*. Remember we mentioned there are hundreds of wineries? Before you go you need to know *where* you are going. If you only have a weekend, pick a stretch of road and only a town or two to visit. If you have longer, you can afford to travel a bit. But either way, you will need to focus in on your desired regions/

wineries you'd like to experience. There are so many things to see in both Napa and Sonoma, so we suggest picking one area, then making plans for another trip or two. Trust us, the wine country is worthy of several visits.

2. *Make reservations.* Not all wineries are open to the public, but of the ones that are, some require reservations. While there are tasting rooms at wineries that have regular hours, many wineries are by appointment only so we suggest making a reservation wherever you can. Some wineries can have varied hours and varied days that they are open, so it's best to plan ahead with appointments so you aren't disappointed when you arrive. There'll be plenty of wineries, and if you plan correctly, you will be able to hit a couple in a day.

3. *Budget for costs.* A majority of the wineries in Napa and Sonoma charge a tasting fee. It's not outrageous, but usually ranges from $5-$15 per winery. Though some are more. So if you plan on visiting a dozen wineries, the price can add up. The good news is that some wineries will waive the tasting fee if you buy a bottle of wine. That's what you're there for anyways, right? So take advantage of it and be sure to have some room in your budget to buy some bottles and pay a few tasting fees. A note: there are some wineries that do not charge tasting fees. However, it is courteous to buy a bottle of their wine if you are impressed. At least that's our feeling. You are going to be blown away by how good these wines are.

4. *Plan some fun excursions.* Even though we're mostly coming for the wine, there are several other fun activities to be had. The scenery is amazing, so get out and experience it. Picnics are a great way to enjoy the landscape and if you're there during the warmer months we say go for it. Plan on packing up a basket with some great local foods (and wine) so you can enjoy that California sunshine. Also plan on doing some shopping in the local towns, as well as taking in the scenic drives along the rolling hillside and even the Pacific Coast. Napa and Sonoma offer a great regional experience, beyond wine tasting.

5. *Don't forget about the food!* Even though you have wine on the brain, keep in mind that wine is best enjoyed when paired with food (we'll talk a little more on this later). Napa and Sonoma both have some of the best rated restaurants in the country and they use a lot of locally grown foods. Plus, they make it their business to pair delectable dishes with the best wines across the region so you get the best of both worlds. You will want to make sure to visit many local restaurants during your stay, so start researching the highlights of the region. This book has listed some of the best in both Napa and Sonoma to help you.

Share your experiences online at wineopolis.com

When to Go

So when is the best time to go? Honestly, any time is a good time to go. Different seasons have different experiences to offer, and they all offer something great. It's all a matter of preference. Let's talk a bit about the general climate.

California is famed for sunshine and temperate weather. Even though the north can be a touch cooler, sunshine still abounds. In actuality, the wine country weather is very similar to the Mediterranean. The summers are hot and dry and the winters are moist yet mild. Rainfall occurs, though not all too often and it varies across the region. The areas closest to the Pacific Ocean have the least variation in temperature from summer to winter, while the inland valleys are hotter and colder, respectively. This weather makes it ideal for grape growing.

But there are other factors to consider besides weather such as the density of tourists you may encounter as well as harvest times. Next we'll break it down by season so you can decide what appeals to you most.

- *Spring*. Springtime in Wine Country is not to be missed. The landscape is dotted with trees displaying pink and white blooms, the grass is still green, the yellow mustard flowers are out in full force, and the days are not terribly hot. This is the most temperate time of year. One week can be warm and in the 70s, the next week can be cold, rainy and in the 50s. Most room rates are still low before the summer boom, so it's also economical. Springtime is not terribly crowded and it's a good time to experience the region with some fellow wine lovers and still being able to enjoy some solitude during your stay.

- *Summer*. Summer is when the action happens, which also means it can be crowded, though the very hot temps can push some people off until the fall. However, with more visitors to Wine Country, there is a boost in activity, with more events to entertain larger crowds during the season. It is this time of year that the grapes are full grown and are quite a sight as they glisten on the vine. The summertime typically brings very hot days (sometimes in the 100s), but the nights are cooler, usually in the 60s. Room rates are higher, mostly because it's the time of year when most people *can* travel. So, you'll likely have to share the sights with a few more people on the wine tour circuit but there are many great things to see and do outdoors during this season.

- *Autumn*. Autumn is harvest time. As grapes are harvested off the vine you can literally *smell* it in the air. California enjoys an *Indian Summer*, which means September and October can be so warm it still feels like summertime. This makes the fall a great time to take

Share your experiences online at wineopolis.com

in some warm weather. But it also means that autumn is the most popular time to visit the wine country. Rooms can be sold out and the prices are at their highest. It's also a popular time for weddings. When looking to come in the autumn, it's best to book months in advance. Popularity drops off by mid-November as the air starts to get cooler, which means rates start to drop as well.

- *Winter*. Wintertime is the least crowded time, but that doesn't mean it's lacking in fun. Temperatures are cool for California, with days in the 40s -50s. It's also the rainy season, so outdoor activities can be a challenge. However, it is the quietest time by far making it a great romantic getaway when you want to be left alone. The best part about the winter in Wine Country is the price. Winter rates are the lowest of the year and you can find many good deals on hotels and bed & breakfasts. Less people also means more personalized attention at the wineries. So it's a great season if you are serious about wine and want a little one on one attention.

There's a perfect season to fit travel to Wine Country. Whether you're looking to mingle with wine loving tourists or need a quiet getaway, a visit to Napa or Sonoma won't disappoint any time you go. Before we start exploring the wineries, it's a good idea to get a little information about wine tasting so you can get the most out of your experience. Next, we'll talk about wine tasting basics, flavors of the region and the foods you'll want to pair with your wine.

II. A Brief Study on Wine Tasting

Okay, so you may be thinking, I like to drink wine, what more do I need to know? Bottle to glass to mouth...no problem! Well, whether you're a novice, expert or wine fanatic, the quest involves more than just drinking. Each visit to Wine Country is a learning experience for everyone. Getting to know more about the wine you are enjoying enhances your experience. Being able to take a sip and share with friends what you're tasting and what you like about the wine is like finding a fun new way to communicate.

A Few Wine Terms to Know

Let us start with some basic wine-ology. Wine is made when grapes ferment (with the help of yeast). The grapes are crushed, releasing the juice, which then sits for a period of time. The sugar then turns into alcohol which means you now have wine from those grapes. But in your quest to be a true wine connoisseur, you will need to know a little bit more. Here are some basic terms you will want to be familiar with.

Basic Wine Terms:

- *Varietal* – denotes the type of grape that is used for a wine, usually giving the wine its name. (Merlot, Pinot Noir and Chardonnay for example).
- *Tannins* – a group of chemicals found naturally in plants. Grape skins and seeds contain tannins. When wine is fermented with the seeds and skins, the tannins enter the wine thus making it more dry or bitter tasting. Red wines contain high amounts of tannins, while white wines are low (having not been fermented with any skin or seeds).
- *Appellation* – a geographic area where grapes are grown (usually regulated by a governmental body).
- *Tasting Flight* – a term used by wineries to describe a specific selection of wines chosen for sampling and comparison.
- *Tasting Note* – The written description from a wine taster about a wine's taste, aroma, body, acidity and texture.

Now that you have some of the lingo down, let's move on to wine tasting! There is a bit of an art to tasting wine, but it's easy. Here we go.

How to Taste a Wine

Wine tasting can be defined as the examination of wine using the senses. Some people just consider how a wine *tastes*. But there actually is a lot more going on! Wine tasting seeks to heighten all of the senses by noting the look, smell and feel as well as the taste. Tasting also allows us to learn more about the wine-making process, how each varietal is grown and produced, and also learn more about the region in which the grapes are grown. Wine tasting rooms are run by employees of the winery who are there to answer all questions and to take you on the journey from vine to bottle to the wine you're about to sip from your glass.

Before we break down the tasting process, let's paint a picture of a wine tasting room. Most wineries have tasting rooms set up so visitors can sample a variety of the winery's featured wines and specialties. When you step into a tasting room, you will line up behind a counter and will be given a list of the wines available to taste. There will also be a dump bucket available. This is for spitting or dumping out wine from your glass. Most serious wine drinkers don't swallow all of the wines they taste. In fact, they may often take a sip or two, spitting each of those out and then dumping the rest of the pour when they are done. You can certainly consume each pour, but you might get a bit tipsy after the first three glasses. And then how can you experience more wines? It's completely acceptable to spit out the wine after you have swirled it

Share your experiences online at wineopolis.com

in your mouth to experience the feel and taste. This way you keep your senses about you. And believe it or not, you can actually taste just as much about the wine on the way out than on the way in.

Steps to tasting a wine:

1. *Observe the wine in the glass.* After you are served, hold the glass up to the light and notice the color and consistency. A really good wine is typically deeper in color at the bottom with the color fading more towards the top. Make sure to keep your fingers on the stem of the glass and away from the bowl of the glass itself. Your fingers around the glass can warm the wine and even change the taste. Plus, it doesn't look as sophisticated.

What personality does your wine have?

Just like people, wines can have different personalities, though we're not talking about exactly the same thing. There are several terms wine connoisseurs use to assign certain attributes to wines. Here are a few favorites:

- **Textures & Tannins** – Tannins can make a wine dry, but they also help wines age. And when they age, they gain complexity and richness. Try to determine the level of tannins in any wine you taste.

- **Flavors & Aromas** – No too wines smell alike. Usually we attribute natural smells to wine, like fruits, flowers, herbs and woods. What we smell can even influence what we taste, even though it still just grapes. Aromas and flavors are often unique to each person and after enough practice, your sense of smell and taste will become more developed to detect and describe those flavors and aromas.

- **Dryness** – Dry wines aren't really *dry,* they just aren't as sweet tasting as other wines. A very dry wine or "bone dry" is when most of the sugar has converted to alcohol and there is very little sweetness (like a Chianti).

- **Oakiness** – Wine is usually fermented in oak barrels or just aged in oak barrels. Either way, some level of oak will seep into the wine. Some wines carry this flavor more than others. Some love a little oak, others not so much. We say it depends on the wine.

- **Finish** – Finish refers to how long the taste of the wine lingers in your mouth after your sip. With some wines the taste is gone the second you swallow (or spit) while others stay around a bit.

Share your experiences online at wineopolis.com

2. *Swirl the wine.* As you are holding the glass, swirl the wine around a few times. A wine with a high alcohol content will leave some lines (called legs) along the edge of the glass as the wine swirls, while lighter wines will swirl cleanly.
3. *Smell first*! Before you drink you need to smell. Tip the glass towards you and stick your nose inside. Try to determine what aromas you smell. Don't get frustrated. The more you do this, the better you will get. If a beginner, ask the attendant what smells you should be looking for and then try to determine if you can make them out. Wines can have different aromas, be it floral, citrus, woody, earthy or metallic. Once you get good at it, you'll smell the difference between different varietals and it will only enhance what you taste.
4. *Now sip.* Once you've sniffed, you can sip. Take a medium sized sip and allow the wine to swirl around your mouth a few times. Try to see what tastes you pick up that you did or didn't smell. Pick out any flavors you can and then either swallow or spit it out into the dump bucket.
5. *Notice the aftertaste.* After the wine has left your mouth, the experience isn't over. See how long the taste lingers. Some wines are crisp and have no lingering taste, while others can remain for a while, thus increasing your enjoyment. You can take other sips if you like, but if you are ready for the next wine, pour the remainder of your glass into the bucket. (Nobody's feelings will be hurt. It's part of the process.)

Congratulations. Now you know the basic tips in wine tasting so you'll look like a pro whether you are one or not. Now it's time to talk about food!

Pairing Wine with Food

What makes a good wine great is often the food it is served with. If you don't believe us now, you soon will. When wine tasting, on top of learning about wine, you'll also be learning about what foods go best with the wine you are tasting. There are some generic "rules", such as lighter wines with lighter dishes, heavy wines with heavy dishes. But there really is a lot more to it. Here are some of the basics for you to consider when deciding what wine to order with your meal.

Wine & Food Pairing Suggestions:

- *Sweet wines go with sweet meals.* There is a reason we have *dessert* wines. They go with dessert. Simple, but important nonetheless.
- *Fruity wines go with salty foods.* If you have a very salty dish, especially salt-water seafood, then pair it with a fruity white wine like a Sauvignon Blanc.

Share your experiences online at wineopolis.com

- *White wines go with (most) seafood.* Sort of an addition to the above, when eating seafood, whether it's scallops, shrimp or any type of white fish, pair it with a Chardonnay, Riesling or Sauvignon Blanc.
- *Full bodied wines go with rich foods.* When you are having a very heavy, rich dish such as beef or lamb or just a rich sauce, then you should choose a rich red wine such as a Cabernet Sauvignon. Strong flavors are best complimented with strong wines.
- *Spicy foods need a light, fruity wine.* A very sweet and fruity wine, like a Riesling or Gewurztraminer, will help counteract spiciness.
- *Smoked foods need a low tannin red wine.* When having smoked duck or any type of smoked meat, choose a rich wine low in tannins (making it is less dry) like a Merlot.

Keep in mind that these are more guidelines than actual rules. It really boils down to your preference. The only reason we make suggestions is so you have a balance. A good pairing will allow the wine to bring out the best flavors of a food and vice versa. When you are tasting wines, take the opportunity to ask the attendant about what foods that specific variety will go best with and then try it out when you buy a bottle. Also everyone in restaurants around Napa and Sonoma will be able to recommend a good wine for all of their dishes, so take them up on their advice. You'll have a great meal.

Best Flavors of the Region

Food is a big deal in Wine Country. A *big deal.* Maybe it's because San Francisco is just a hop, skip and a jump away and it prides itself on haute cuisine. Or maybe it's because the region is surrounded by farmland and has some of the best fresh fruits and vegetables to be found. Either way, restaurants in Napa and Sonoma are excellent. Below are just a few of the foods that are grown locally.

- *Fresh fruit.* Both Napa and Sonoma are known for fresh peaches, cherries, apples and plums, just to name a few. Don't miss out on trying them all or the many great jams and jellies sold in many local shops.
- *Cheeses.* California has a lot of cows, which means there's also a lot of cheese. Cheese is one of the best pairings for wine and Wine Country has no shortage of gourmet cheeses, both local and imported.
- *Breads.* Brick oven breads and pizzas are common throughout the region, so don't pass up the bread basket at local restaurants. Chances are, the breads are fresh and made locally. Bread is also perfect for eating with cheese and wine – a classic wine tasting meal.

Share your experiences online at wineopolis.com

- *Olives*. Olives are abundant in Wine Country. You'll spot groves of olive trees at many wineries given the Mediterranean climate. This means, there's plenty of olive products to enjoy such as tapenades, spreads and our favorite – olive oil.
- *Meat & Seafood*. There are plenty of livestock in the region and the locally grown beef is renowned for its quality. In addition, the nearby Pacific Ocean offers a great variety of fresh seafood. Be sure to ask what is grown or caught locally and taste it any chance you get.

Next let's talk about how to get all of this good stuff back home.

Don't Go Home Empty Handed! (Bringing Wine Back)

If you're going to go wine tasting, be prepared to buy some wine. Easier said than done, right? What to do with all those bottles? It's not like you'll be stuffing them all in your suitcase for the trip home (although we'd be lying if we said we haven't done it ourselves). The best bet is to plan on having some wine shipped back to your house. Luckily, most wineries are prepared for this and have many options available for sending their wines across the state or across the globe.

Most wineries are prepared to ship your order straight to your home. You will, however, have to consider the rules of your state or country and any taxes they might impose. And it's not likely they'll do it for just one bottle. (That, we're afraid, you'll be stuffing in your suitcase unless you drink it on your trip – not a bad idea). If you decide to purchase a case of a certain variety, or even a case of many varieties, then these are easily shipped.

Almost all wineries have wine clubs. By joining a wine club program, you can sign up for having a different wine sent to your home each month. For wineries where you are impressed with their collection, this is a great idea. It also makes for a great gift. Prices are reasonable and it ensures you can enjoy the wine all year long. Plus, wine club members always get discounts when buying wine or even at the winery itself.

Another option is to check the wine on your flight in its own packing box. Most wineries have heavy duty cardboard boxes (for a price) that will allow you to pack your bottles and check them as luggage. They will stay fairly protected and you won't have to wait for a shipment to arrive at your house.

For the serious wine collector who may want to buy many wines from many wineries, it will be very expensive to ship a case at a time from each winery. If this is the case, you can look into a third-party shipper who will package everything together for you and charge a bulk price. Third-party shippers can be found in most cities across the region or you can ask the staff at any number of wineries for their personal recommendation. You are buying their wine after all, so they will be more than helpful.

So now we know how to taste, how to pair our wine with food, and we know how to get all that wonderful wine back home. Without further ado, it is time to explore Napa.

Share your experiences online at wineopolis.com

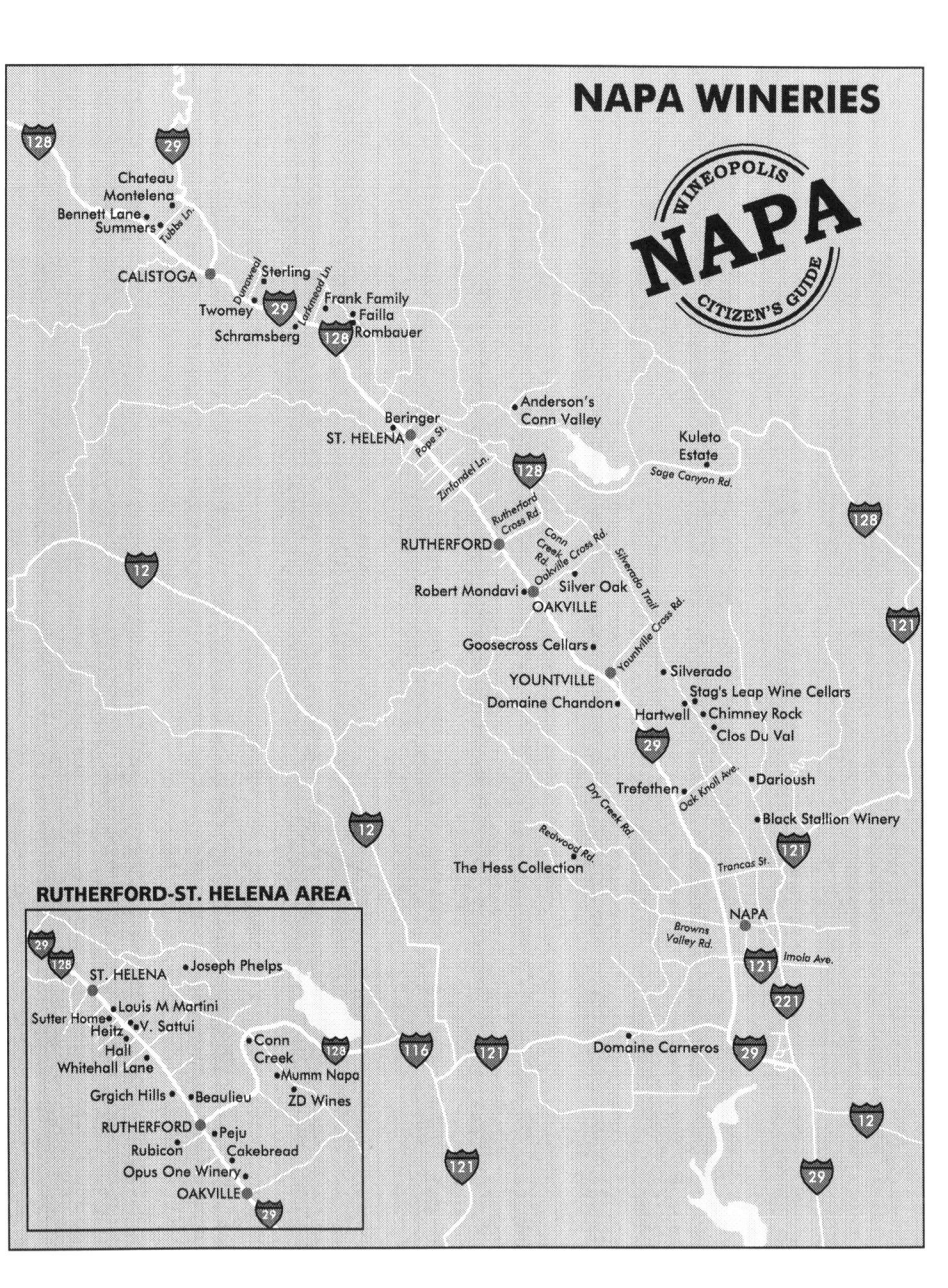

III. Experiencing Napa

Now it's time to explore Napa Valley in all its beauty. We'll go about it in the following manner: a brief highlight of towns and appellations, a listing of our top recommended wineries, then a listing of recommended restaurants, the top things to see and do, and finally recommendations on where to stay. Makes sense to us.

> Here is one thing to keep in mind – what's great about Wineopolis is that we grow based upon the experiences of the community at large. And while we have tried to list the best places in this guide book, if you don't see your favorites listed here or if you want to share a new discovery with your fellow travelers and wine lovers, go to www.wineopolis.com here your voice can be heard! Now, let's get started.

All About Napa

Napa County is long and thin stretch of land that is roughly thirty miles long and less than five miles wide. This is because the valley is actually in-between two small mountain ranges. To the west, lies the rugged Mayacamas Range and to the east are rolling hills of the Vaca Range. Most of the towns and wineries in Napa County can be found along Highway 29 and running parallel, the Silverado Trail. Both of these roads stretch up through the narrow valley and are easy to navigate.

Highway 29 has typically been known for the larger production wineries while the Silverado Trail has more of the boutique wineries for you to visit. Either way, both routes make for fantastic wine exploration. The Napa Valley is home to some of the most fertile soil to be found in the state, which means it grows some fantastic grapes. We'll start at the southern end of the valley and work our way north, describing the towns and appellations that are found along the way. Let's start with the (few) towns to be found in Napa.

Napa

The town of Napa has the highest population to be found in the county at nearly 75,000 people. That number is continuing to grow, however. Napa has some great bed & breakfasts, as well as some historic areas of town dating back to the mid-1800s. The main drag in the town of Napa is Soscol Avenue, which has several modern retail and restaurant chains and the usual tourist traps. The real fun is to be found in the surrounding areas of town and even downtown which has been going through some extensive upgrades lately. There's a great mixture of well-known hotel resorts as well as small local hotels and B&Bs sure to fit the taste of any traveler.

Yountville

Just north of Napa lies Yountville. This town is named after local legend George Yount (remember him from earlier?). Though very small in population, barely over 3,000 people, this town is big on fine dining. There are several upscale, top of the line eateries in Yountville making it a popular destination for foodies. This town thrives on visitors to the wine country, so there is not one amenity you'll find lacking when you stay here.

St. Helena

Nearing the middle of the valley lays St. Helena. Pronounced He-LAY-na, this town is as picturesque as it gets. Filled with immaculately preserved Victorian style houses, well-manicured streets and lawns, with not one piece of litter to be found, it's practically a theme park. Located in the heart of the valley, St. Helena is near many famous vineyards and has some excellent restaurants as well.

Calistoga

At the northern tip of the valley lies the town of Calistoga. Though a little more rugged than St. Helena, Calistoga has a lot to offer. Besides

Share your experiences online at wineopolis.com

wineries, there are two mineral water producers centered here: Calistoga and Crystal Geyser. There are also a few local breweries, such as the Silverado Brewing Co. In addition, Calistoga has developed a reputation as being a great spa getaway featuring healing mud-baths.

Of course, there are several other spots on the map, such as Rutherford and Oakville, as well as some smaller outlying communities sprinkled throughout the valley. We'll come across those when we start profiling the best wineries of the region. Next, let's look at the appellations within Napa County.

Napa Appellations

Napa Valley is home to some of the most prestigious wines in the world. When you see an appellation from Napa, you know it is usually a good quality wine. Napa Valley is itself an appellation, with 15 sub-appellations across the region. Below is a list of the appellations to be found in Napa (in alphabetical order) so you can determine which ones you want to visit or look for in your local wine shop. They're all dynamite grapes, to be sure, but you may learn to prefer some regions over others.

Napa Valley AVA – Napa Valley has its own appellation, though it refers to grapes mostly grown in the southern region of the valley. It will pretty much encompass any grapes officially grown in Napa that are not a part of the other 15 appellations.

Atlas Peak AVA – Atlas Peak is located up in the hills above the valley floor towards the center of the county. It is known for fruity Cabernet Sauvignon and Chardonnay.

Calistoga AVA – This region was just approved in December of 2009 after six long years of consideration. It is located in the northern part of the Valley near the town of Calistoga and grapes here are mostly for Cabernet Sauvignon, Zinfandel, Syrah and Petite Sirah.

Chiles Valley District AVA – Chiles Valley is also elevated above the Napa Valley floor in the hills towards the northeastern end of the valley. It is known for Cabernet Sauvignon and Merlot with black-cherry flavors.

Diamond Mountain District AVA – Diamond Mountain is in the northwest, in a higher elevation than nearby Calistoga. Grapes here are used for rich Cabernet Sauvignon and Cabernet Franc, as well as full-bodied Chardonnay.

Howell Mountain AVA – Located in the northern part of the valley above Calistoga, the climate is drier than the valley floor. Grapes grown here are Cabernet Sauvignon, Merlot, Zinfandel, as well as less fruity Chardonnay.

Share your experiences online at wineopolis.com

> **Why appellations are so important to wine enthusiasts.**
>
> As you explore the wineries, you will hear a lot of talk about appellations, climate, temperatures, soil make-up, etc., called *terroir**. For wines, the flavors and aromas you detect as you sip are all features of the grape. And what influences the grape is the region in which it is grown. If you like a more fruity Chardonnay versus a dry, earthy Chardonnay, then it helps to learn more about the appellations and the resulting style of wines that are produced from those areas to find the type of wine you like.
>
> *Another word to know: *terroir* – This French word is used to describe all of the geographic and climate factors affecting grapes such as the soil, temperature, topography of the land, amount of moisture and amount of sunlight.

Los Carneros AVA – Located in the valley in the southwestern part of the county, with temperatures being cooler due to the Pacific Ocean winds, this area is known for Pinot Noir, Merlot as well as Chardonnay.

Mount Veeder AVA – Above Los Carneros in the hills, this appellation is known for grapes that age well. The area grows Cabernet Sauvignon, Merlot, Zinfandel, as well as Chardonnay.

North Coast AVA – This is a very broad California appellation that covers 6 counties, including Napa. Since this appellation also covers many smaller appellations with much more recognizable names, most wines will carry the name of the sub-appellation.

Oak Knoll District AVA – Located just below Yountville in the central part of the valley. Grapes here have a longer growing season than most other areas and the reds have a spiciness as well as fruity tones. It is known for Merlot, Cabernet Sauvignon, as well as Chardonnay.

Oakville AVA – Oakville is also on the central valley floor just north of Yountville. Region is known for Cabernet Sauvignon, Merlot as well as Sauvignon Blanc.

Rutherford AVA – Above Oakville lays Rutherford, which has slightly higher temperatures than other valley floor regions. This region is famous for its Cabernets (Sauvignon and Franc) which are earthy in flavor.

Spring Mountain District AVA – Located in the hills north of Mt. Veeder, Spring Mountain has cooler temperatures most of the year. This region produces reds that are higher in tannins, as well as Chardonnay and Viognier that are less fruity than those wines produced with grapes from the valley floor.

Share your experiences online at wineopolis.com

St. Helena AVA – Located on the valley floor towards the northern end of the valley, this region is protected from the cooler Pacific winds by the hills to the west. Grapes grown here are Cabernet (Sauvignon and Franc), Merlot, Zinfandel and Chardonnay.

Stags Leap District AVA – Stags Leap is just to the east of Yountville at a slightly higher elevation. The area is known for cherry-flavored Cabernet Sauvignon, Merlot and Sangiovese, as well as fruity Chardonnay and Sauvignon Blanc.

Wild Horse Valley AVA – Located on the very tip of the valley in the southeast, Wild Horse Valley also has cherry-flavored Cabernet Sauvignon and Sangiovese, though more acidic than those in Stags Leap. Chardonnay here has a distinctive pear flavor.

Yountville AVA – Yountville is in the central part of the valley. This region is best known for Cabernet and Merlot with floral aromas and heavy tannins.

As you can see, most appellations in Napa are known for Cabernet Sauvignon, Merlot and Chardonnay. But don't be fooled by all the appellations listed above. In reality, Napa wines only account for a small percentage of the total wine production in the state of California. But, since Napa has some of the best tasting wines in the State, it is one of the top destinations for all wine lovers.

So now it is time for our favorite part…the wineries. Get ready to start marking those (or all) you want to visit.

Share your experiences online at wineopolis.com

Napa Wineries: A Guide

We're going to highlight the best wineries in the region. And that's saying something, because they are *all* excellent. But we only have so much time (and so many pages) so we're picking the favorites and those not to be missed. We'll go through the list geographically, starting in the southern tip of the valley and moving north. Now we can't list every great winery in the region, so if you have a favorite that we've missed then come online and tell us about it at Wineopolis.com!

> **A quick note on how our listings are organized. We will first list the winery, its address and contact information, appellation (if known), followed by a brief description of the winery, their tasting room days, hours and fees (if any), the best wines they have to offer and any interesting features or facts. Even though a lot of wineries are open daily, almost all are closed on major holidays so always check with them before you visit.

Domaine Carneros

1240 Duhig Road, Napa, CA 94559 / 800-716-BRUT (2788)
www.domainecarneros.com
Appellation: Los Carneros
Hours: 10am – 6pm daily (Tours daily 11am, 1pm, 3pm)
Tastings: $7-15 per glass or $15 for three wines

Domaine Carneros is partnered with Taittinger and Kopf who are famed for sparkling wines in France. Therefore, this winery is known for its Vintage Brut, as well as a Brut Rosé. The building is built in honor of the Taittinger Chateau in Champagne, France and brings a little French sophistication to the countryside. Besides sparkling wines, this winery also has a zesty Pinot Noir. They charge by glass or by tastings, but the cost is well worth it as this winery has a true French ambience. Service is inside or out on the terrace overlooking the countryside – a view not to be missed.

The Hess Collection Winery

4411 Redwood Road, Napa, CA 94558 / 707-255-8584
www.hesscollection.com
Appellation: Napa Valley, Mt. Veeder
Hours: 10am – 5pm daily
Tastings: $10-20 per person

Founded by Donald Hess, Swiss millionaire and art collector, this winery could also serve as a modern art museum. So, you get culture *and* great wine at the same time. They have a good Chardonnay, Sauvignon Blanc, Zinfandel

make notes in your Wine Log at the end of this section

and Cabernet Sauvignon. The art collection is open daily and can be toured in conjunction with the winery. They also have food and wine pairing sessions available by reservation on Thursday, Friday and Saturday at 10 am and 2 pm.

Trefethen Vineyards

1160 Oak Knoll Avenue, Napa, CA 94558 / 866-895-7696
www.trefethen.com
Appellation: Oak Knoll
Hours: 10am – 4:30pm daily
Tastings: $10-25 per person

Trefethen is a family owned vineyard that also places a high importance on environmentally sustainable practices. So it's green, too! They are best known for their Dry Riesling, Chardonnay, Merlot and Cabernet Sauvignon. The modern-day winery was built on the same grounds as the old Eshcol winery dating back to the late 1800s. The original building is still in use, making this winery a perfect blend of past and present.

Black Stallion Winery

4089 Silverado Trail, Napa, CA 94558 / 888-279-6272
www.blackstallionwinery.com
Appellation: Oak Knoll
Hours: 10am – 5pm daily
Tastings: $10 per person or $30 per person for reserve wines

This winery is one of the newest along the famous Silverado Trail. This winery used to be an equestrian center and still keeps some of that spirit. There is an indoor tasting room, as well as tastings on the outdoor patio, which is right up against a "petting vineyard" where you can handle the grapes. These wines are sold only online and at the vineyard, so make sure to visit. Black Stallion is known for Cabernet Sauvignon, Merlot, Chardonnay, Muscat, as well as a great Meritage blend.

Darioush

4240 Silverado Trail, Napa, CA 94558 / 707-257-2345
www.darioush.com
Appellation: Napa Valley, Mt. Veeder, Oak Knoll
Hours: 10:30am – 5:30pm daily
Tastings: $25 per person or reservations for private tableside tastings available

Darioush is a standout along the Silverado trail as it resembles a Persian palace more than a winery. Made from travertine stone straight out of Iran

Share your experiences online at wineopolis.com

and sporting 16 enormous columns leading up to the winery entrance, this building is a visual wonder to behold. The red wines here are known for being similar to the rich French Bordeaux blends. The winery is also renowned for their Cabernet Sauvignon and Shiraz.

Clos Du Val

5330 Silverado Trail, Napa, CA 94558 / 800-993-9463
www.closduval.com
Appellation: Napa Valley
Hours: 10am – 5pm daily
Tastings: $10 for estate wines (waived upon wine purchase), $20 for reserve wines

Clos Du Val is a French name, which translates as "small estate of a small valley." However, there's nothing small about it. This winery's specialty is its Cabernet Sauvignon, but they do have a very good Chardonnay and Pinot Noir as well. There is a lovely outdoor court as well as picnic areas, so this is the perfect winery for an afternoon picnic (in good weather, of course). To taste reserve wines is more expensive, but that also includes a souvenir glass complete with winery logo. Do not miss this winery if you can help it.

Chimney Rock Winery

5350 Silverado Trail, Napa, CA 94558 / 800-257-2641
www.chimneyrock.com
Appellation: Stag's Leap
Hours: 10am – 5pm daily
Tastings: $20-30 per person

This winery boasts Dutch-inspired architecture, replete with a pristine white building and scalloped edges. Get ready for their hearty Cabernet Sauvignon (a specialty) which packs a nice punch. The winery also makes a good Fumé Blanc and a Cabernet Sauvignon-Merlot-Petit Verdot blend they call Elévage.

Stag's Leap Wine Cellars

5766 Silverado Trail, Napa, CA 94558 / 866-422-7523
www.cask23.com
Appellation: Stag's Leap
Hours: 10am – 4:30pm daily
Tastings: $15-30 per person

Stag's Leap is another winery known for its Cabernet Sauvignon. Their estate grown Cabernet is labeled CASK 23 S.L.V. (thus the name of their website). In fact, it was the 1973 Stag's Leap Cabernet Sauvignon that beat four other

Which wines did you taste?

ROMBAUER VINEYARDS

3522 Silverado Trail, St. Helena, CA 94574 / 707-963-5170
www.rombauer.com
Appellation: Napa Valley
Hours: 10am – 5pm daily
Tastings: $10 per person by appointment

Rombauer Vineyards is a family-owned winery whose roots go all the way back to the German winemaking region of Rheingau. Koerner Rombauer, formerly a commercial airline captain, first bought property here in 1972 because he wanted his family to escape the city life and enjoy a family upbringing. He also wanted to go back to his roots of winemaking, thus he began planting vines and making his own label years later in 1982. You'll perhaps be familiar with Koerner's great aunt Irma Rombauer, who wrote *The Joy of Cooking*. The inspiration of food, paired with wine, has remained a family tradition and today almost every family member participates in the winery.

The winery itself is located just off Napa's famous Silverado Trail and is nestled in a forest of pine trees. The California ranch-style main house at first glance looks as if it is part of the landscape, most of it ensconced in vines and shrubs. There is a great long porch where you can sit and enjoy your wine while you take in the views of the valley below. Down the gravel path from the house, you'll encounter beautiful pockets of roses, tulips and azaleas with whimsical bronze sculptures peering out amongst them.

The tasting room here is open daily from 10am to 5pm and is $10 per person. Appointments are advised, though they are not required. You'll want to taste their Carneros Chardonnay, Merlot, Napa Valley Cabernet Sauvignon and Zinfandel. Around the room, you'll find a lot of trinkets and memorabilia from Koerner Rombauer's life, including many signed photographs from the scores of celebrities, dignitaries and notable personalities who have visited the winery over the years.

We would also suggest you take a tour of the winery (available by appointment) where you can see a double-horseshoe shaped cellar built in 1997 that goes deep underground into the hillside.

...tell your friends at wineopolis.com

French wines in the infamous blind taste test held in France in 1976, now called "The Judgment of Paris." So you'll definitely want to taste the Cab.

Hartwell Vineyards

5795 Silverado Trail, Napa, CA 94558 / 800-366-6516
www.hartwellvineyards.com
Appellation: Stag's Leap
Hours: Monday – Saturday Appointment Only
Tastings: $25 for 4 wines, $45 for flight paired with cheeses

This vineyard is planted on top of a 4-million year old volcano (and today thankfully dormant). Hartwell Vineyards is a worthy stop to taste their Sauvignon Blanc, Merlot and Cabernet Sauvignon. Tastings are by appointment only, but that means if you plan ahead, you'll have a great time without a crowd. And you'll be treated with a glass of Sauvignon Blanc at the door, taken on a private tour and treated like a very special guest. So definitely make an appointment.

Silverado Vineyards

6121 Silverado Trail, Napa, CA 94558 / 707-257-1770
www.silveradovineyards.com
Appellation: Napa Valley
Hours: 10am – 4:30pm daily
Tastings: $10 estate wines, $20 reserve wines

Silverado Vineyards has a very Tuscan feel and with buildings of warm terracotta, stone, and stucco you'll feel like you have traveled to the Italian countryside. This vineyard is perched on a hilltop overlooking the sprawling vineyards below. They also offer a library wine and food pairing upon appointment which includes four Cabernet Sauvignons from different vintages (years) paired with a variety of foods. Definitely sign up for it, as Cabernet Sauvignon is their specialty. Another interesting note, this winery is owned by Walt Disney's daughter Diane Disney Miller, so there's sure to be a magical feel and dedication to service.

Domaine Chandon

1 California Drive, Yountville, CA 94599 / 800-736-2892
www.chandon.com
Appellation: Varied
Hours: 10am – 5pm daily (excluding major holidays)
Tastings: $16-22 per person depending on flight

Domaine Chandon (also the name of the founder) is California's first French-owned winery. Domaine is son to Moet-Hennessey, so tradition is strong

where did you go?

TWOMEY CELLARS

1183 Dunaweal Lane, Calistoga, CA 94515 / 800-505-4850
www.twomeycellars.com
3000 Westside Road, Healdsburg, CA 95448 / 800-505-4850
Appellation: Napa Valley, Russian River Valley
Hours: 9am – 4pm Monday-Saturday
Tastings: $5 per person (includes complimentary glass)

Twomey Cellars (pronounced Too-Me) prides itself on its Merlot. Merlots have somewhat fallen in popularity in recent years, especially in the region, but this Merlot still ranks at the top of the list of fabulous Merlots. However, don't think that's all they make. In recent years, Twomey has expanded and also offers a Pinot Noir and Sauvignon Blanc, both very good and worth tasting.

The flagship winery is located near Calistoga in the northern end of the valley, not far from the historic Silverado Trail. You'll see two matching white cottages adjacent to one another in the midst of rolling vineyards. When you taste here it's only $5 and you get a complimentary glass (we miss those). There are tours available, but by appointment only.

Just recently Twomey purchased land in the Russian River Valley just outside of Healdsburg in Sonoma County. They have a tasting room there as well, so no matter where you're touring, this winery should be an option. The tasting room here is ultra-modern and has multiple windows through which you can admire the expanse of vineyards outside.

But it really all comes back to their Merlot. This wine is smooth and fruity, with slight plum and oak flavors. Some might even detect in it a hint of chocolate. The Merlot grapes they plant are small yet intensely flavored. Thanks to the morning fog, these grapes are allowed to ripen slowly, even further enhancing the strong fruit characteristics of the grape. The winemaker, Daniel Baron, has perfected the slow decanting technique of soutirage traditional, which is what allows the Merlot to be clear, brilliant and maintain its fruity quality. This is a Merlot you must really taste for yourself and see what flavors and aromas you experience.

log it, blog it, share it at wineopolis.com

at this winery. The tasting room, called Le Salon, includes complimentary hors d'oeuvres to accompany their tastings. Their specialty is their sparkling wine so we suggest the Reserve Tasting at $18 per person. They also have a restaurant at the winery, Étoile, offering lunch and dinner so it's a great excursion. If you come on the weekend, they have tours of the winery every hour on the hour. Be sure to also check out their brandy and pear liqueur that are both made on site.

Goosecross Cellars

1119 State Lane, Yountville, CA 94599 / 800-276-9210
www.goosecross.com
Appellation: Varied
Hours: 10am – 4:30pm daily
Tastings: No price listed, call ahead to reserve

Goosecross Cellars have a great variety of wines, to be sure, especially the Chardonnay and Cabernet Sauvignon. But what we love best about this vineyard is that they offer a Goosecross Wine Basics class on Saturday mornings in the summer. You can learn all about wine and how to taste it, while tasting some pretty good ones in the process. You can reserve either by phone or through their website. The class is free and also includes a winery tour. Works for us.

Silver Oak Cellars

915 Oakville Crossroad, Oakville, CA 94562 / 800-273-8809
www.silveroak.com
24625 Chianti Road, Geyserville, CA 95441 (Alexander Valley/Sonoma)
Appellation: Napa Valley, Alexander Valley
Hours: 9am – 4pm Monday-Saturday
Tastings: $10 per person (includes complimentary glass)

Silver Oak is famous for their Cabernet Sauvignon and people travel here from all over to taste it at this one-of-a-kind vineyard. When the vineyard releases a new wine, which they do every February, connoisseurs line up outside, literally. This Cab is so popular, it is all they produce. They are all Cabernet Sauvignon all the time. There is a second winery in Alexander Valley in Sonoma, though each location has its own distinct Cab. If you can, visit them both. You must not miss these wines.

what did you see?

RUBICON ESTATE

1991 St. Helena Highway, Rutherford, CA 94573 / 800-RUBICON
www.rubiconestate.com
Appellation: Rutherford, Napa Valley
Hours: 10am - 5pm daily
Tastings: $25 guest fee (includes tour and tasting of five wines)

Rubicon Estate is the brain child of famous filmmaker Francis Ford Coppola. While that may be reason enough for most to visit this estate (and we'd agree) it also has some fascinating features and very good wines.

The estate was formerly the Niebaum Estate. Back in 1879, Finnish Sea Captain Niebaum invested his vast fortune into this estate for the purpose of making wine. What followed was called Inglenook. The beautiful chateau was modeled after his favorite houses in the French countryside. In subsequent years, however, the estate fell short of its former greatness. Coppola first purchased land here in 1975 and made some wine, but it wasn't until nearly 20 years later that he began purchasing the rest of the land, winery and vineyard thus reuniting most of the original Niebaum Estate.

Today, thanks to the purchase by Coppola, the chateau is meticulously maintained, the winery has been updated and the entire estate is now called Rubicon. The name, it turns out, was chosen by Coppola in reference to Caesar's march on Rome and his subsequent crossing of the Rubicon River which stands as the "point of no return." The estate was in disarray before Coppola and the renaming in 2006 has helped establish the new vision of the winery.

When visiting Rubicon you are, in essence, entering as a guest to learn about the wine you are tasting. The specialty here is the Rubicon, which is a Cabernet Sauvignon, Merlot and Cabernet Franc blend. To visit, you purchase a guest pass (only $25) that includes a wine tasting and is good for three days, so you can keep coming back. And trust us, there's more to do here than just sip. For starters, there's the Centennial Museum (showcasing the history of the estate) as well as the Mammarella Wine Bar where you can sit and enjoy any number of wines by the glass. There are also a number of tours all available by appointment that will take you around the chateau (you can even see some of Coppola's movie props).

post your trip photos at wineopolis.com

Robert Mondavi Winery

7801 Highway 29, Oakville, CA 94562 / 888-766-6328
www.robertmondaviwinery.com
Appellation: Oakville, Napa Valley
Hours: 10am – 5pm daily
Tastings: $15 per person for three wines in tasting room

Robert Mondavi is what helped turn Americans on to California wine. Therefore it's no surprise that this is perhaps the most well-known winery in Napa. Robert Mondavi Winery continues to draw the crowds, for good reason. Their Cabernet Sauvignon Reserve and Fumé Blanc Reserve are excellent. Also, this winery offers more than wine. Throughout the year, there are cultural events, art exhibits, and concerts as well as their very informative winery tours (by appointment). Don't leave Napa without visiting here.

Opus One Winery

7900 St. Helena Highway S., Oakville, CA 94562 / 707-944-9442
www.opusonewinery.com
Appellation: Oakville
Hours: 10am – 4pm daily
Tastings: $30 per person, by appointment only

Opus One is on our list because it started as a partnership between two big names in winemaking: Robert Mondavi and Baron Philippe de Rothschild. The winery has only one wine – Opus One – that's a hefty $180 per bottle. But it is an excellent red wine blend (mostly cabernet sauvignon) and you can taste it for much less. They also have winery tours, by appointment, with a wine tasting at the conclusion for $35 per person. It's worth it for just a taste.

Peju

8466 Highway 29, Rutherford, CA 94573 / 800-446-7358
www.peju.com
Appellation: Napa Valley
Hours: 10am – 6pm daily
Tastings: $10 per person (applicable to purchase)

Peju is a small winery run by the Peju family located in the heart of the valley. The architecture is French Provencal and the vibrant flower beds are a sight to be seen. They are known for their Cabernet Franc and Cabernet Sauvignon, the latter having won many awards. Tours are also available by appointment.

sniff, taste, blog, repeat

CAKEBREAD CELLARS

8300 St. Helena Highway, Rutherford, CA 94573 / 800-588-0298
www.cakebread.com
Appellation: Varied
Hours: 10am – 4pm daily
Tastings: $15 per person, appointment required

Cakebread Cellars was founded by the Cakebread family back in 1973 and they've been producing award winning wines ever since. Now they have grown to encompass 13 different locations over Napa Valley, but it all began at the winery in Rutherford, making it a location definitely worth checking out.

Cakebread Cellars is perhaps best known for their Chardonnay and Cabernet Sauvignon. But, they also have noteworthy Zinfandel, Syrah and Pinot Noir.

They have a wide variety of tastings available, though they all require an appointment so be sure to plan ahead. For $15 per person, you can taste their current release wines. But you may want to dig a little deeper. Their library tasting is $35 per person and is a seated tasting amongst a small group; therefore you really get a lot of attention and information. They also offer a red wine tasting at $30 per person, which is a great deal since they are known for some really great reds, especially the Cabernet Sauvignon. So if Cab is King in your book, we recommend the Vertical Cabernet Sauvignon tasting. For $25, you can taste three different vintages of their winning Cabernet that all hail from the Napa Valley appellation. It's the perfect opportunity to taste how a wine can age over time.

They also have some tastings that incorporate a tour of the property. For $40 per person, you can enjoy a wine and food pairing experience that will also encompass a quick 30 minute tour. You'll then be guided through four food dishes paired with wine. For those of you learning about wine for the first time, Cakebread has a Sensory Evaluation Experience for $30, where you will be educated on aromas and how to train your palate to determine different aspects like residual sugar, alcohol, acidity and tannin.

No matter what tasting experience you choose, you're sure to have a grand time. And you may discover a new favorite wine in the process.

Share your experiences online at wineopolis.com

Rubicon Estate

1991 St. Helena Highway, Rutherford, CA 94573 / 800-RUBICON
www.rubiconestate.com
Appellation: Rutherford, Napa Valley
Hours: 10am - 5pm daily
Tastings: $25 guest fee (good for three days; includes tour and tasting of five wines)

This winery was purchased by famous film director Francis Ford Coppola back in 1975 and he has beautifully maintained the Victorian architecture of the property. The main house was built by Finnish captain Gustave Niebaum who also founded Inglenook winery (a very famous California wine). Coppola since renamed the estate Rubicon, thus the specialty here is the Rubicon (a Cabernet Sauvignon, Merlot and Cabernet Franc blend). The guest fee is good for three days and includes valet parking, access to the chateau, a tour and a tasting of five wines. There are many other educational tours offered and you can even see some props from Coppola's best-known films.

Zd Wines

8383 Silverado Trail, Napa, CA 94558 / 800-487-7757
www.zdwines.com
Appellation: Rutherford
Hours: 10am – 4:30 pm daily
Tastings: $10-15 per person

ZD Wines is known for great Chardonnay, Pinot Noir and Cabernet Sauvignon. So good, in fact, they have been served to three different U.S. Presidents. The name ZD comes from the initials of the owners (Zepponi and deLeuze) as well as standing for an aerospace term "Zero Defects". Shows how much they value quality control and it shows in the wine. A great stop.

Mumm Napa Valley

8445 Silverado Trail, Rutherford, CA 94573 / 707-967-7700
www.mummnapa.com
Appellation: Napa Valley
Hours: 10am – 5pm daily
Tastings: $10 and up depending on flight

Mumm is a premier name in sparkling wines and they have three great Bruts, the Blanc de Blancs, Blanc de Noir, and Brut Prestige. They also have a vintage sparkling wine called DVX. Mumm Napa Valley was founded by both G.H. Mumm of France and Joseph E. Seagram from America. The tasting room is behind a wall of glass overlooking the beautiful vineyard and the

what did you like?

BENNETT LANE WINERY

3340 Highway 128, Calistoga, CA 94515 / 877-629-6272
www.bennettlane.com
Appellation: Napa Valley
Hours: 10am – 5:30pm daily   **Tastings: $10 per person**

North of Calistoga, as you head towards the mountains you will stumble across Bennett Lane Winery. It's a smaller winery, with a small production, but the wines here are as stellar as the backdrop. When you venture here, you will be driving through some of the most rural and un-touched land in all of Napa.

The winery was purchased a few years ago by Randy and Lisa Lynch and they have already made a name for themselves with their Cabernet Sauvignon and blend of Cabernet, Merlot and Syrah they call Maximus. Named after a second century Roman General who apparently had a love of wine just as he had a love of war. They also have a White Feasting Wine Maximus, which is a blend of Chardonnay, Sauvignon Blanc and Muscat.

You won't find a lot of frills here. The tasting room is simple and elegant tended by very warm and friendly staff. There's an outside terrace, too, where you can admire the views. The Lynch's were the first wine owners to own a NASCAR team. But you'd never know they were diehard fans from seeing the winery until you stumble across the emblazoned Ford model they keep on display.

Tastings here are $10 per person for a flight of five wines. They do have daily tours available by appointment. But even better, they offer a blending session for parties of six or more called the Varietals Fruit Flavor Custom Blend Experience. During this session, you'll get to learn about blending and then try your own hand at creating a custom blend. First, you'll take a tour of the "petting vineyard" where you will learn about the soil and how grapes grow. You'll get to touch the different varietals (and even taste a few grapes during harvest.) Then you go inside and try your hand at blending. Afterwards, you'll get to take home your own specially-made bottle and enjoy a wine and cheese pairing afterwards. The cost is $200 per person, but it's an opportunity to really get to experience winemaking hands-on.

let us know your favorites at wineopolis.com

winery is renowned for its excellent tour. This winery also features several photography galleries housing a mixture of famous and local photographers. These galleries are a must see, so be sure to stop here.

Beaulieu Vineyard

1960 St. Helena Highway S., Rutherford, CA 94573 / 800-264-6918
www.bvwines.com
Appellation: Rutherford
Hours: 10am – 5pm daily (except major holidays)
Tastings: $10-20 per person depending on tasting

Also known as BV, Beaulieu Vineyard was founded in 1900 by Georges de Latour, making it the oldest continuously operating winery. The winery makes a whole host of great wines, including Chardonnay, Pinot Noir, Cabernet Sauvignon, and Sauvignon Blanc to name a few. However, the real collector's wine is the Georges de Latour Private Reserve Cabernet Sauvignon. Check out the website for a number of "premium services" that are available (for a price) such as two-for-one passes, tours and reserve tastings.

Grgich Hills Estate

1829 St. Helena Highway, Rutherford, CA 94573 / 800-532-3057
www.grgich.com
Appellation: Napa Valley
Hours: 9:30am – 4:30 pm daily
Tastings: $10 per person

The specialty wine at Grgich is the Chardonnay. The vineyard was started by Mike Grgich and Austin Hills of Hills Brothers Coffee. Grgich found fame when his Chardonnay from Chateau Montelena won in a blind taste test in Paris in 1976 (yep, that famous "Judgment"). After partnering with Hills, they started the Grgich Hills Estate. The Chardonnay is a smooth, buttery and simple delight so don't miss a chance to sample it.

Cakebread Cellars

8300 St. Helena Highway, Rutherford, CA 94573 / 800-588-0298
www.cakebread.com
Appellation: Varied
Hours: 10am – 4pm daily
Tastings: $15 per person, appointment required

Cakebread Cellars encompasses 13 locations all over Napa Valley; however their first location is the winery in Rutherford. Even though they require appointments for their tastings, they have a wide variety of personalized tastings to choose from. Their library tasting is $35 per person and is a seated tasting amongst a small group; therefore you really get a lot of attention and information. They

find free resources at wineopolis.com

TREFETHEN VINEYARDS

1160 Oak Knoll Avenue, Napa, CA 94558 / 866-895-7696
www.trefethen.com
Appellation: Oak Knoll
Hours: 10am – 4:30pm daily
Tastings: $10-25 per person

Trefethen is a family-owned winery in the Oak Knoll AVA region of Napa Valley. They can proudly say that they do not buy one single grape outside of this appellation to produce their wine. This winery has stayed in the family since its inception in 1968 when the lands were purchased by husband and wife Eugene and Katie Trefethen. They bought the old Eshcol winery that had long ago fallen into disrepair. However, the original building was restored and is still being used today. It is in this building where you can find the tasting room, wine library and wine aging barrels.

The winery has nine different varietals: Chardonnay, Cabernet Sauvignon, Merlot, Riesling, Pinot Noir, Cabernet Franc, Malbec, Petit Verdot, and Viognier. Our favorites include the Riesling, Chardonnay and Cabernet Sauvignon, but you can be the judge about which wine speaks to you the most. To help your decision, just know that in 1979 it was a Trefethen Chardonnay that earned the title of "Best Chardonnay in the World" at a tasting event in Paris, France. Make sure you try it.

We also like that this winery is committed to environmentally-sustainable practices. The family sees themselves as stewards of the land. After all, they've been here for over 40 years. For their operation, they use biodiesel fuels and they don't use chemicals. When you drink a Trefethen wine, keep in mind all of the love and care that went into its creation.

When you visit here, tastings are $10 per person or $25 per person if you wish to try their Reserve wines. They do have tours of the winery available by appointment. And the event that's really exceptional is the Twilight at Trefethen. For $100 per person, you can experience an exclusive night at the winery, complete with a wine, cheese and charcuterie reception. You'll then take an exclusive tour of the winery and then taste an aged Cabernet Sauvignon straight from the barrel. It's a fun night to be had.

make notes in your Wine Log at the end of this section

also offer a red wine tasting at $30 per person, which is a great deal as they are known for their reds, especially the Cabernet Sauvignon.

Conn Creek Winery

8711 Silverado Trail, St. Helena, CA 94574 / 707-963-9100
www.conncreek.com
Appellation: Napa Valley
Hours: 11am-4pm Monday-Friday, 10am-4pm Saturday
Tastings: $10 per person for six wines, $25 for Cabernet Sauvignon flight

Conn Creek is easily found at the intersection of Silverado Trail and Rutherford Road. You can't miss its Mediterranean-style stucco building. The winery, founded by a former submarine officer, gets its name from a nearby creek that flows through the vineyard. This winery has a limited production and their specialty is the Napa Valley Cabernet Sauvignon, as well as a Bordeaux-style blend called Anthology.

Anderson's Conn Valley Vineyards

680 Rossi Road, St. Helena, CA 94574 / 800-946-3497
www.connvalleyvineyards.com
Appellation: Napa Valley
Hours: 10am – 5pm daily
Tastings: complimentary for current release wines, but by appointment only

Tucked away in a small valley outside of St. Helena lies Anderson's Conn Valley, a family-owned vineyard. Tours are always run by a member of the family, and it's a great way to get a real behind-the-scenes look at a winery and ask a lot of questions. They are known for their Cabernet Sauvignon, as well as their Pinot Noir and Chardonnay.

Hall St. Helena Winery

401 St. Helena Highway S., St. Helena, CA 94574 / 866-667-4255
www.hallwines.com
Appellation: Rutherford
Hours: 10am – 5:30pm daily
Tastings: $15 per person for four wines, $25 for Estate Cabernet tasting

The Hall Winery was founded by husband and wife team Craig and Kathryn Hall, who are in the process of building a new multi-million dollar facility. Oh, and by the way, this facility is being designed by avant-garde architect

Share your experiences online at wineopolis.com

ROBERT MONDAVI WINERY

7801 Highway 29, Oakville, CA 94562 / 888-766-6328
www.robertmondaviwinery.com
Appellation: Oakville, Napa Valley
Hours: 10am – 5pm daily
Tastings: $15 per person for three wines in tasting room

Even if you're not a self-proclaimed wine expert, we'll bet money you've heard of Robert Mondavi or at least tasted their wine. Named for founder Robert Mondavi, this winery has been going strong for over forty years. They have since produced some iconic wines, the best being the reserve Cabernet Sauvignon and Fumé Blanc. In fact, the latter is a Mondavi creation after combining Sauvignon Blanc with Sémillon for a drier white wine. Mondavi has been at the forefront of innovation, be it a new form of cold fermentation, new stainless steel tanks, and even utilizing NASA for areal imaging of the vineyards to determine vine health.

In fact, Robert Mondavi has been so prevalent in winemaking, they are a huge reason why Americans, and others around the world, have gotten to know California wines so well. So it's only fitting that a visit to Napa should include visiting this winery. There's a lot more going on here than just wine. The winery holds several events throughout the year. There is a summer festival concert series held outdoors, as well as occasional art exhibits that are held on the grounds.

The building itself is an homage to the Spanish-style missions that once dominated the land. Dotted along the grounds are many sculptures by local artist Beniamino Benvenuto Bufano.

You have a few options when visiting here. The first is a wine tasting of three wines for $15 that is held in the tasting room. There's also a guided tasting and/or food and wine pairing. Tours are where you'll get to see the on-site caves, as well as the picnic area. There's a gift shop where you can buy any number of wine books among other souvenirs. But for those who want a full hands-on experience, take the To Kalon tour and tasting. You will get a chance to experience the winemaking process from grape to cellar to final product. There are many other tours available, but you will need appointments for all of them. Check their website for available times.

Which wines did you taste?

Frank Gehry; so it's sure to stand out. The new facility is scheduled to open sometime in 2010. But in the meantime, you can visit the existing winery and taste their great line of red wines including a Cabernet Sauvignon, Merlot and Cabernet Franc.

V. Sattui Winery

1111 White Lane, St. Helena, CA 94574 / 800-799-2337
www.vsattui.com
Appellation: Varied
Hours: 9am – 6pm (Spring, Summer, Fall), 9am-5pm (Winter)
Tastings: $5 classic tasting, $10 premium tasting

V.Sattui Winery is known for its expansive grounds which make for a perfect afternoon picnic among the rows of shade trees. But don't worry if you didn't pack your picnic basket ahead of time, as there is a marketplace and deli, as well as a barbeque and pizza bar nearby. They also offer food and wine pairings at the tasting bar Monday – Thursday, 11am – 5pm. And don't forget the wine. This winery produces several varietals, such as their Rosé, sparkling wine, Merlot, Zinfandel and Chardonnay, so plan a day of it and try a few with a bite of food.

Whitehall Lane Winery

1563 St. Helena Highway, St. Helena, CA 94574 / 800-963-9454
www.whitehalllane.com
Appellation: Rutherford
Hours: 11am – 5:45pm daily
Tastings: $12 per person

This winery was purchased by current owner Thomas Leonardini in 1993, making it one of the newer kids on the block. But since then they have garnered a reputation for great wine, including their Merlot, Sauvignon Blanc, Pinot Noir and Cabernet Sauvignon. The building is bright yellow and of a more angular/modern design, making it a standout in the local community. The rooms are bright and spacious, leaving plenty of room to sip the wine and enjoy the view.

...tell your friends at wineopolis.com

CLOS DU VAL

5330 Silverado Trail, Napa, CA 94558 / 800-993-9463
www.closduval.com
Appellation: Napa Valley
Hours: 10am – 5pm daily
Tastings: $10 for estate wines (waived upon wine purchase), $20 for reserve wines

Clos Du Val is French for "small vineyard estate of a small valley" though in actuality it's not what we'd call small. You will feel like you have hopped on over to the French countryside. Not surprising as owner John Goelet has French roots, as well as his partner Bernard Portet (from a family of winemakers).

What first put this winery on the map was when its 1972 Cabernet Sauvignon was picked as one of only six wines to compete against French wines in a 1976 wine tasting, since dubbed "The Judgment of Paris". Even though the Cab didn't win, the distinction of being selected helped propel Clos Du Val to the top of every wine drinker's list.

The winery is located in the Stag's Leap district of Napa and the specialty here is Cabernet Sauvignon. However, you will also be pleased with their Chardonnay, Merlot, and Pinot Noir. You can partake in their tasting of estate wines for $10, though this price is waived upon a wine purchase. For $20 you can taste their reserve wines. Once here, you can tour the demonstration vineyard and learn about different trellising techniques and how to identify different Merlot varietals.

The winery itself is very picturesque. Following the lined drive filled with cypress trees, you come upon the vine covered building. In the background are the peaks of Stag's Leap and directly in front is a charming Mediterranean garden. On the grounds is also an olive grove, where you are welcome to picnic so be sure to pack a basket and reserve your table ahead of time (they tend to go fast). They also have a Pétanque court (which is a French style of bocce ball) that you are welcome to play. There are tours available by appointment, but you will need to call the winery ahead of time to check availability.

The winery is near many other Napa attractions such as the Napa Valley Museum and the Napa Valley Opera House.

where did you go?

Heitz Wine Cellars

436 St. Helena Highway South, St. Helena, CA 94574 (Tasting Room)
500 Taplin Road, St. Helena, CA 94574 / 707-963-3542
www.heitzcellar.com
Appellation: Napa Valley
Hours: 11am – 4:30 pm daily (tasting room hours)
Tastings: Complimentary!

Finally, one of the (few) wineries left that have complimentary wine tastings. Heitz Wine Cellars has their tasting room separate from the actual winery. However, if you'd like to see the winery as well, you'll need to call for an appointment. They have been known for their Chardonnay, but in recent years their Cabernet Sauvignon has been gaining in popularity and acclaim. Try them both.

Kuleto Estate

2470 Sage Canyon Road, St. Helena, CA 94574 / 707-963-9750
www.kuletoestate.com
Appellation: Napa Valley
Hours: Appointment Only
Tastings: $35 per person for a tour, four wines and cheese pairing.

Kuleto Estate is another winery known for its Cabernet Sauvignon and the building has a very distinct Italian Villa feel. But there's another good reason to visit. The Kuleto Estate has a ranch (pigs, goats, cattle, among other livestock) as well as fruit orchard, organic garden and even several ponds filled with farm raised fish. Therefore, it's worth the tour and tasting.

Sutter Home Winery

277 St. Helena Highway S., St. Helena, CA 94574 / 707-963-3104
www.sutterhome.com
Appellation: Varied
Hours: 10am – 5pm daily (Visitors Center)
Tastings: Complimentary!

Sutter Home has a big reputation which is warranted as they sell a lot of good wine. This winery has a visitors center that is open daily so you can just drop by without making a reservation. Tastings are complimentary, the gift shop is open and you can do a self tour of a White Zinfandel garden. Yes, they are known especially for their White Zin, which was a creation by the Trincheros family that has owned the winery since 1947. But besides that, there are several other great wines to taste.

log it, blog it, share it at wineopolis.com

DARIOUSH

4240 Silverado Trail, Napa, CA 94558 / 707-257-2345
www.darioush.com
Appellation: Napa Valley, Mt. Veeder, Oak Knoll
Hours: 10:30am – 5:30pm daily
Tastings: $25 per person or reservations for private tableside tastings available

When coming to Darioush Winery, you may feel as if you have stumbled upon a Persian palace with its 16 stone columns lining the front entryway. In fact, the stone used for the palace and columns was quarried in the region of Persepolis (the capital of ancient Persia) which is now in modern-day Iran. Owner Darioush Khaledi grew up in a Shiraz-growing region in Iran, which is where his passion for wine began as his father used to make wine as a hobby. Once in America, Darioush purchased land in Napa and Darioush's dream of owning a winery was fulfilled after partnering with winemaker Steve Devitt.

What this winery excels at are rich red wines, from the Bordeaux blends, to the Cabernet Sauvignon and Shiraz. Though they have some quality whites as well including a Chardonnay and Viognier. The main tasting is $25 per person and there are some tours available by appointment. However, there are some exclusive engagements that are worth mentioning. First is a fine wine and artisan cheese tasting for $50 that encompasses a tour of the facility as well as a wine tasting paired with many hand-crafted local and other hard-to find cheeses from around the world. This happens every day at 2pm and you'll need to call ahead for an appointment.

If you are looking for a more in-depth adventure, then try the Quintessential Wine Experience. After enjoying champagne and caviar, you get to descend into Darioush's private wine cellar where you can browse his private selection and choose a bottle. Then you'll enjoy it alongside the Estate Cabernet Sauvignon (a treat) along with some gourmet food dishes. It's $300 per person, but très gourmet. For a little less, there's an invitation only tasting which is a trip into the wine cellar where you can taste the exclusive reserve wines along with some specially prepared hors d'oeuvres. Whatever level of experience you are searching for, you can find it here.

what did you see?

Beringer Vineyards

2000 Main St., St. Helena, CA 94574 / 707-963-4812
www.beringer.com
Appellation: Napa Valley
Hours: 10am – 5pm (Winter), 10am – 6pm (Summer)
Tastings: $10 tour fee includes two wines or $5 for three wines; $5-16 for reserve wine flights

Beringer Vineyards is a must-see for anyone traveling to Napa. The beautifully preserved Germany-inspired Rhine House, built by Jacob and Frederick Beringer in the late 1800s, faces the road and beckons you inside. There are several tours of the property available for a variety of prices, so it's best to call ahead and make a reservation. The winery also has a series of hand-carved wine aging tunnels that are available for tours. But the best attraction, by far, is the house. Oh, and the Private Reserve Chardonnay and Cabernet Sauvignon.

Louis M. Martini Winery

254 St. Helena Highway S., St. Helena, CA 94574 / 800-321-WINE
www.louismartini.com
Appellation: Varied
Hours: 10am – 6pm daily
Tastings: Complimentary, small fee for reserve wines

Wine tastings at Louis M. Martini Winery are best done outside in "Martini Park", a shaded terrace overlooking the grounds. They offer at least ten different wines year round in the tasting room, including their famous Moscato Amabile. Tours are available by appointment. This winery was once dubbed a "Napa Valley Gem" and once you visit, you'll see why. Also try their excellent Cabernet Sauvignon and Petite Sirah.

Failla

3530 Silverado Trail North, St. Helena, CA 94574 / 707-963-0530
www.faillawines.com
Appellation: Napa Valley
Hours: 10am – 5pm daily by appointment
Tastings: $10 per person

Failla is a great winery to visit if you'd like a change of pace. The winery itself is like an old farmhouse, nestled amongst the trees just off Silverado Trail. The walls are of knotted pine and the large stone fireplace just invites you to come sit, relax and sip some wine. The tasting room is really nothing more than a large living room, so you really get an intimate, quaint and laid-back feel. Make sure to try the Chardonnay, Pinot Noir and Syrah when you visit.

post your trip photos at wineopolis.com

THE HESS COLLECTION WINERY

4411 Redwood Road, Napa, CA 94558 / 707-255-8584
www.hesscollection.com
Appellation: Napa Valley, Mt. Veeder
Hours: 10am – 5pm daily
Tastings: $10-20 per person

The Hess Collection Winery was started by Swiss entrepreneur Donald Hess. He initially purchased vineyards on Mount Veeder back in 1978. So, years later when he decided to try his hand at operating a winery, he already had some of the most fertile and well-producing vineyards for Cabernet Sauvignon in Napa. When he found the nearby Christian Brothers Mont La Salle property for sale, he knew he had a golden opportunity before him and The Hess Collection Winery subsequently opened to the public in 1989.

The winery building itself, a historic stone building coated with vines, dates back to 1903 when it was first built by Colonel Theodore Gier. The winery produces wine from almost 310 acres across Mount Veeder at differing elevations, but most of them pretty steep. This unique terroir allows the Cabernet Sauvignon grapes to develop a very rich and bold character, thus creating very unique wines. This winery has an exceptional Cabernet Sauvignon as well as a very good Chardonnay.

Donald Hess seeks to preserve the land and farms the vineyards using sustainable practices, his motto being, "Nurture the land; return what you take." Another interesting fact about Donald Hess is that he's an avid modern art collector. So much so, in fact, that he has a modern art collection available for viewing at the winery. His collection consists of hundreds of paintings and sculptures by many contemporary artists from across the globe. The art gallery is open daily for self guided tours.

To taste the Hess current release wines, the cost is $10 per person in the tasting room (reserve wines are $20). Or if you'd like, there is a current release wine and cheese pairing for $25 per person by reservation only. There is a tour of the museum plus wine tasting, which we recommend, for $35 per person during the week and $40 per person on the weekend. You will need to call ahead for times and a reservation.

sniff, taste, blog, repeat

Joseph Phelps Vineyard

200 Taplin Road, St. Helena, CA 94574 / 707-967-3720
www.jpvwines.com
Appellation: Napa Valley
Hours: 9am – 5pm Monday-Friday, 10am – 4pm Saturday and Sunday
Tastings: $20 per person (for six wines) by appointment

The folks at Joseph Phelps Vineyard are stewards of the land. They strive to preserve and ecologically enhance the vineyard and surrounding environment. So they make great wines, responsibly. The winery also has an amazing terrace overlooking the sloping grounds and nearby lake, an area called Spring Valley. The surrounding grounds are abundant with wildlife, from beehives, to jackrabbits and quail that are free to roam. Try their Insignia label, which is a blend of Cabernet Sauvignon and other Bordeaux-style grapes, all grown locally.

Rombauer Vineyards

3522 Silverado Trail, St. Helena, CA 94574 / 707-963-5170
www.rombauer.com
Appellation: Napa Valley
Hours: 10am – 5pm daily
Tastings: $10 per person by appointment

You may know Irma Rombauer as the author of The Joy of Cooking. But before they were famous in culinary circles, the Rombauer ancestors were known for winemaking in the Rheingau region in Germany. Koerner Rombauer first bought property here in 1972 and began making his own label years later in 1982. The specialty wine here is the Diamond Selection Cabernet Sauvignon. Many celebrities have visited the winery and you can see signed photographs by many of them in the tasting room.

Frank Family Vineyards

1091 Larkmead Lane, Calistoga, CA 94515 / 800-574-9463
www.frankfamilyvineyards.com
Appellation: Napa Valley
Hours: 10am – 5pm daily
Tastings: Complimentary!

Another great vineyard for sparkling wines, Frank Family Vineyards is also considered a "Point of Historical Interest." The interest being the stone building that was the Historic Larkmead Winery first erected back in 1884.

Share your experiences online at wineopolis.com

It has since been refurbished, but when you walk around the property you can feel the history of the area. Despite the sparkling wines, the winery also has some excellent Chardonnay and Cabernet Sauvignon. And there is a great little picnic spot behind the historic stone building. Tours are available by appointment.

Twomey Cellars

1183 Dunaweal Lane, Calistoga, CA 94515 / 800-505-4850
www.twomeycellars.com
Appellation: Napa Valley
Hours: 9am – 4pm Monday-Saturday
Tastings: $5 per person (includes complimentary glass)

Attention Merlot lovers: this is the winery for you. Twomey (too-me) Cellars has devoted all its energy to bottling a top of the line Merlot, although now they also offer a good Pinot Noir and Sauvignon Blanc. But at the Calistoga winery location, Merlot is still king. You can enjoy your wine in vintage-styled cottages overlooking the vineyard. Tours are offered Monday-Friday, and Saturday by appointment.

Sterling Vineyards

1111 Dunaweal Lane, Calistoga, CA 94515 / 800-726-6136
www.sterlingvineyards.com
Appellation: Varied
Hours: 10:30am – 5pm Monday-Friday,
10am – 5pm Saturday-Sunday
Tastings: $20 per person admission for aerial tram, self-guided tour and wine tasting

Sterling Vineyards is more like a theme park than a winery, although there are plenty of good wines, too. The winery sits atop a hilltop that you access by aerial tram. Sounds like an amusement park, but it's a winery, we assure you. Once you reach the top, you'll get panoramic views of Calistoga and the northern valley so it's well worth the visit. The winery itself is fashioned after the Greek Island of Mykonos thereby the building is of pristine white stucco. The winery is also completely modern, having motion sensitive DVD screens that allow you to take a self-guided tour of the facility along the many balconies and pathways. Come here for the experience, as well as the Chardonnay and Cabernet Sauvignon.

what did you like?

Chateau Montelena

1429 Tubbs Lane, Calistoga, CA 94515 / 707-942-5105
www.montelena.com
Appellation: Napa Valley, Calistoga
Hours: 9am – 4pm daily
Tastings: $20-40 per person

This vineyard has an award-winning Chardonnay – a victor at the "Judgment of Paris". Yep, this is the Chardonnay that won the blind taste test in 1976 and Chateau Montelena has been a popular destination ever since. The winery looks like an ancient castle perched atop a hill and in fact dates back to the late 1800s, though it remained dormant for decades until the early 1970s. The property also has a man-made lake (Jade Lake) and an adjacent Chinese garden that provide perfect tranquility for tasting wine. You have to come here to taste that award winning Chardonnay, though they have a great Riesling, too. Oh and there's a Bottle Shock tour for $40 where you can see all of the behind-the-scenes locations used in the movie.

Recommended Viewing: *Bottle Shock* (2008)

This recent movie is based on a true story about the rise of American wine (and more specifically Northern California wines) and its respected reputation. The movie centers on a blind wine taste test which pitted American wines against French wines in Paris in 1976. It's now referred to as the "Judgment of Paris." The American wines won, of course, but it's a great journey featuring Chateau Montelena winery and how a Napa Chardonnay beat the infamous French.

Summers Estate

1171 Tubbs Lane, Calistoga, CA 94515 / 707-942-5508
www.summerswinery.com
Appellation: Napa Valley
Hours: 10:30am – 4:30pm
Tastings: $7 per person (applicable to wine purchase)

Summers Estate is located just north of Calistoga and is the second vineyard for owners Jim and Beth Summers, the first being just over in Sonoma. At this vineyard they cultivate "old vine" Charbono (a dark red with high tannins), Zinfandel and Cabernet Sauvignon grapes. They have a fabulous Estate Charbono, as well as a good reserve Zinfandel. Charbono is a rarity in California and Summers Estate produces this varietal.

let us know your favorites at wineopolis.com

Bennett Lane Winery

3340 Highway 128, Calistoga, CA 94515 / 877-629-6272
www.bennettlane.com
Appellation: Napa Valley
Hours: 10am – 5:30pm daily
Tastings: $10 per person

Bennett Lane Winery is off the beaten path, located a ways off the main roads up towards the mountains. But, the trek is worth it. Not only will you be traveling through some rural landscapes, mostly untouched by man, you will experience a great hidden gem in Napa. The signature wine here is Maximus, named after a Roman emperor, which is a fantastic Cabernet Sauvignon, Merlot and Syrah blend. When in a group of 6 or more, you can take part in a "blending" session, where you get to try your hand at blending different wines and develop your own creation. The winery is also a great place for a picnic, so make it a day trip.

The Schramsberg Caves: An experience you shouldn't miss

If you are planning on visiting Napa, then you must make plans to visit the Schramsberg Winery. First for their amazing sparkling wines and second to tour and experience their 120 year-old underground caves.

In 1862, German-born Jacob Schram purchased land on the mountain slopes in Napa Valley with the intent of moving his family there, clearing the land, building a home and planting grapes. Wine was his passion and he was anxious to start winemaking. To help escape the intense heat of the California summer, he (along with many Chinese workers) began digging into the mountainside and creating a series of caves. These cool underground cellars were perfect for storing and aging wine.

As the years passed, the log cabin was replaced with a lavish Victorian house and the small family-run operation turned into a booming business. Today, you can visit these beautifully maintained and preserved caves. There are almost two miles of tunnels to be explored! They provide the perfect opportunity to get a glimpse of winemaking up close and personal, so plan a visit to these underground cellars with a great guide who will give you a hands-on tasting after exploring the Schramsberg history together.

Schramsberg Vineyards / 1400 Schramsberg Road, Calistoga, CA 94515 / 800-877-3623
Tour Reservations: (707) 942-4558
Go exploring and share your visit with the rest of us at Wineopolis!

find free resources at wineopolis.com

Wine Log: My Wine Notes

Winery: _____

Wine: white   red   rosé   sparkling

Name: _____

Vintage: _____

Varietal: _____

Price: _____

Body:	Simple	Moderately Complex	Complex
Acidity:	Low	Medium	High
Sweetness:	Dry	Off-dry	Sweet
Finish:	Short	Moderate	Long

Aromas & Flavors:

Whites/Roses

Citrus	Lemon, Grapefruit, Orange, Tangerine
Tree Fruit	Pear, Apple, Apricot, Peach, Nectarine
Tropical	Melon, Pineapple, Passion fruit, Banana, Mango
Floral	Geranium, Violet, Rose, Orange Blossom,
Herbal	Sage, Mint, Tea, Cut green grass
Mineral	Stone, Slate, Flint, Chalk
Spicy	Cinnamon, Nutmeg, Clove, Spiced Apple, Ginger
Nutty	Walnut, Almond, Hazelnut
Woody	Vanilla, Oak, Toast, Coconut
Yeast	Baked Bread, Bread Dough, Pie Crust
Caramel	Butter, Honey, Caramel, Butterscotch, Crème Brûlee
Other	Fuel/Diesel

Reds

Berry	Blackberry, Raspberry, Strawberry, Blueberry
Tree Fruit	Red Cherry, Black Cherry, Plum
Dried Fruit	Raisin, Fig, Prune, Berry Jam
Floral	Geranium, Violet, Rose
Herbal	Bell Pepper, Olive, Eucalyptus, Mint, Sage
Earth	Mushroom, Mineral, Forest floor
Meat	Smoked Meat, Bacon, Leather
Spice	Cinnamon, Clove, Black Pepper, Licorice/Anise
Woody	Vanilla, Oak, Cedar, Toast, Charred Wood, Tobacco
Caramel	Chocolate, Mocha, Molasses, Honey, Butterscotch
Other	Pencil Lead, Tar

Notes: _____

_____

_____

Rating

1	2	3	4	5
Don't Like It		It's Okay		I Love It!

Share your experiences online at wineopolis.com

Wine Log: My Wine Notes

Winery: _____
Wine: white   red   rosé   sparkling
Name: _____
Vintage: _____
Varietal: _____
Price: _____

Body:	Simple	Moderately Complex	Complex
Acidity:	Low	Medium	High
Sweetness:	Dry	Off-dry	Sweet
Finish:	Short	Moderate	Long

Aromas & Flavors:

Whites/Roses

Citrus	Lemon, Grapefruit, Orange, Tangerine
Tree Fruit	Pear, Apple, Apricot, Peach, Nectarine
Tropical	Melon, Pineapple, Passion fruit, Banana, Mango
Floral	Geranium, Violet, Rose, Orange Blossom,
Herbal	Sage, Mint, Tea, Cut green grass
Mineral	Stone, Slate, Flint, Chalk
Spicy	Cinnamon, Nutmeg, Clove, Spiced Apple, Ginger
Nutty	Walnut, Almond, Hazelnut
Woody	Vanilla, Oak, Toast, Coconut
Yeast	Baked Bread, Bread Dough, Pie Crust
Caramel	Butter, Honey, Caramel, Butterscotch, Crème Brûlee
Other	Fuel/Diesel

Reds

Berry	Blackberry, Raspberry, Strawberry, Blueberry
Tree Fruit	Red Cherry, Black Cherry, Plum
Dried Fruit	Raisin, Fig, Prune, Berry Jam
Floral	Geranium, Violet, Rose
Herbal	Bell Pepper, Olive, Eucalyptus, Mint, Sage
Earth	Mushroom, Mineral, Forest floor
Meat	Smoked Meat, Bacon, Leather
Spice	Cinnamon, Clove, Black Pepper, Licorice/Anise
Woody	Vanilla, Oak, Cedar, Toast, Charred Wood, Tobacco
Caramel	Chocolate, Mocha, Molasses, Honey, Butterscotch
Other	Pencil Lead, Tar

Notes: _____
_____
_____

Rating

1	2	3	4	5
Don't Like It		It's Okay		I Love It!

...tell your friends at wineopolis.com

Wine Log: My Wine Notes

Winery: _____

Wine: white   red   rosé   sparkling

Name: _____

Vintage: _____

Varietal: _____

Price: _____

Body:	Simple	Moderately Complex	Complex
Acidity:	Low	Medium	High
Sweetness:	Dry	Off-dry	Sweet
Finish:	Short	Moderate	Long

Aromas & Flavors:

Whites/Roses

Citrus	Lemon, Grapefruit, Orange, Tangerine
Tree Fruit	Pear, Apple, Apricot, Peach, Nectarine
Tropical	Melon, Pineapple, Passion fruit, Banana, Mango
Floral	Geranium, Violet, Rose, Orange Blossom,
Herbal	Sage, Mint, Tea, Cut green grass
Mineral	Stone, Slate, Flint, Chalk
Spicy	Cinnamon, Nutmeg, Clove, Spiced Apple, Ginger
Nutty	Walnut, Almond, Hazelnut
Woody	Vanilla, Oak, Toast, Coconut
Yeast	Baked Bread, Bread Dough, Pie Crust
Caramel	Butter, Honey, Caramel, Butterscotch, Crème Brûlee
Other	Fuel/Diesel

Reds

Berry	Blackberry, Raspberry, Strawberry, Blueberry
Tree Fruit	Red Cherry, Black Cherry, Plum
Dried Fruit	Raisin, Fig, Prune, Berry Jam
Floral	Geranium, Violet, Rose
Herbal	Bell Pepper, Olive, Eucalyptus, Mint, Sage
Earth	Mushroom, Mineral, Forest floor
Meat	Smoked Meat, Bacon, Leather
Spice	Cinnamon, Clove, Black Pepper, Licorice/Anise
Woody	Vanilla, Oak, Cedar, Toast, Charred Wood, Tobacco
Caramel	Chocolate, Mocha, Molasses, Honey, Butterscotch
Other	Pencil Lead, Tar

Notes: _____

_____

_____

Rating

1	2	3	4	5
Don't Like It		It's Okay		I Love It!

let us know your favorites at wineopolis.com

Wine Log: My Wine Notes

Winery: _____

Wine: white   red   rosé   sparkling

Name: _____

Vintage: _____

Varietal: _____

Price: _____

Body:	Simple	Moderately Complex	Complex
Acidity:	Low	Medium	High
Sweetness:	Dry	Off-dry	Sweet
Finish:	Short	Moderate	Long

Aromas & Flavors:

Whites/Roses

Citrus	Lemon, Grapefruit, Orange, Tangerine
Tree Fruit	Pear, Apple, Apricot, Peach, Nectarine
Tropical	Melon, Pineapple, Passion fruit, Banana, Mango
Floral	Geranium, Violet, Rose, Orange Blossom,
Herbal	Sage, Mint, Tea, Cut green grass
Mineral	Stone, Slate, Flint, Chalk
Spicy	Cinnamon, Nutmeg, Clove, Spiced Apple, Ginger
Nutty	Walnut, Almond, Hazelnut
Woody	Vanilla, Oak, Toast, Coconut
Yeast	Baked Bread, Bread Dough, Pie Crust
Caramel	Butter, Honey, Caramel, Butterscotch, Crème Brûlee
Other	Fuel/Diesel

Reds

Berry	Blackberry, Raspberry, Strawberry, Blueberry
Tree Fruit	Red Cherry, Black Cherry, Plum
Dried Fruit	Raisin, Fig, Prune, Berry Jam
Floral	Geranium, Violet, Rose
Herbal	Bell Pepper, Olive, Eucalyptus, Mint, Sage
Earth	Mushroom, Mineral, Forest floor
Meat	Smoked Meat, Bacon, Leather
Spice	Cinnamon, Clove, Black Pepper, Licorice/Anise
Woody	Vanilla, Oak, Cedar, Toast, Charred Wood, Tobacco
Caramel	Chocolate, Mocha, Molasses, Honey, Butterscotch
Other	Pencil Lead, Tar

Notes: _____

_____

_____

Rating

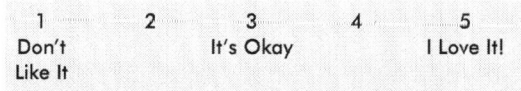

1	2	3	4	5
Don't Like It		It's Okay		I Love It!

Share your experiences online at wineopolis.com

Napa Restaurants: A Guide

Now with all this talk about wine, we shouldn't forget the other important part of the equation: food. Napa has no shortage of fine dining and you won't want to miss the many great eateries and restaurants along the way. There are four-star gourmet restaurants as well as local laid-back hangouts. We'll try to point out the best of every kind in each region so you have a variety of styles and prices to choose from. Below are the top 20 of the region; a very hard distinction as there are dozens more great restaurants but we just don't have the room to list them all. If you have a favorite that we didn't list, then tell us about it at Wineopolis.com!

Like the wineries listed previously, we will start our list with Napa and work our way north up the valley. We'll list the name, address and contact information, price, as well as a brief description of the menu and atmosphere.

PRICE GUIDE (for two entrees only):

$ - Less than $25
$$ - $26-35
$$$ - $36-50
$$$$ - $51 and up

Celadon

500 Main Street, Napa, CA 94559 / 707-254-9690
www.celadonnapa.com
Price: $$$
Hours: Lunch Monday-Friday 11:30am-2:30pm, Dinner 5pm-9pm daily (until 10pm on weekends)
Reservations: Recommended

Touted as "Global Comfort Food", Celadon is a blend of flavors from America, Asia and the Mediterranean and headed by Greg Cole, who also owns nearby Cole's Chop House. Nestled along the Napa River, it has a relaxing atmosphere in the newly revived downtown entertainment area of Napa. Celadon has excellent crab cakes and calamari, as well as a tasty Moroccan-inspired braised lamb shank. They have an extensive wine list, too.

make notes in your Trip Log at the end of this section

Angèle Restaurant & Bar

540 Main Street, Napa, CA 94559 / 707-252-8115
www.angelerestaurant.com
Price: $$$
Hours: 11:30am – 10pm Monday-Sunday
Reservations: Recommended

Angèle is a French Brasserie-style restaurant in Napa's revitalized Hyatt Building Complex downtown. Adjacent to the Napa River, the restaurant offers patio seating so you can take in the view. French food reigns here, the best being the French onion soup, boêuf bourguignon, and a bacon-wrapped veal loin. Angèle is also known for fantastic desserts, the best being their banana gratin with almond crust and vanilla bean ice cream.

Pearl Restaurant

1339 Pearl Street, Suite 104, Napa, CA 94559 / 707-224-9161
www.therestaurantpearl.com
Price: $$
Hours: Lunch 11:30am – 2pm Tuesday-Saturday, Dinner 5:30pm – 9pm Tuesday-Thursday, 5:30pm – 9:30pm Friday-Saturday (Closed Sunday and Monday)
Reservations: Not required

This is the restaurant the locals like to go to, so you know it's good. They boast upscale elegance in a casual atmosphere with generous portions. We're fans. The food has American, Asian, Italian and even Mexican influences. Try the flank steak soft tacos, they're delicious. They also have fresh oysters on the appetizer menu done in all sorts of savory sauces, so come hungry.

Cuvée

1650 Soscol Avenue, Napa, CA 94559 / 707-224-2330
www.cuveenapa.com
Price: $$$
Hours: Dinner 5pm – 9pm Sunday-Thursday, 5pm – 9:30pm Friday-Saturday
Bar hours: 4pm – 10pm Monday-Thursday, 4pm – 10:30pm Friday-Saturday
Reservations: Recommended for the main dining room

Cuvée has a traditional main dining room, but also an outdoor courtyard that's very cozy, so be sure to enjoy dinner here during the warmer months. The bar inside is always inviting and offers a late-night food menu until

Share your experiences online at wineopolis.com

10:30pm on the weekends. The restaurant features some American favorites such as braised short ribs, lacquered BBQ short ribs and pan roasted chicken. They also have a lot of fresh fish from the nearby coast, as well as an extensive list of local wines.

La Toque

1314 McKinstry Street, Napa, CA 94559 / 707-257-5157
www.latoque.com
Price: $$$$
Hours: Dinner 5:30pm - Monday-Sunday
Reservations: Recommended

La Toque is located in the Westin hotel in the heart of downtown Napa. They do offer a prix fixe menu (a set price for a number of dishes) and always use the freshest local ingredients, so you're sure to have a dynamite dish no matter when you visit. This a "dress up" destination on your trip, so bring some nice clothes. The menu is mainly French with some Asian influences. What is really awesome about La Toque is they have a wine pairing menu, so you can try out your new found knowledge about wine.

Ad Hoc

6476 Washington Street, Yountville, CA 94599/ 707-944-2487
www.adhocrestaurant.com
Price: $$$$
Hours: Dinner 5pm – 10pm (except closed Tuesdays and Wednesdays), Sunday brunch 10am – 1pm.
Reservations: Recommended

Right on the sign for Ad Hoc it says "for temporary relief from hunger" – and they couldn't be more right. This restaurant offers family-style dining in a slightly casual, rustic atmosphere. Everyday, they offer a different four-course family-style menu (for a fixed price). If it sounds crazy, perhaps it's because the restaurant was only to be temporary while the owner, Thomas Keller, designed the space for a different purpose. But it became so popular he kept it open. Since every day is different, it's hard to pinpoint a dish but it usually involves a gourmet salad, meat or fresh fish, cheese, fresh bread, and a dessert. The food is amazing, top chef quality and you won't be disappointed.

What did you eat?

Étoile At Domaine Chandon

1 California Drive, Yountville, CA 94599/ 800-736-2892
www.chandon.com
Price: $$$$
Hours: Lunch 11:30am – 2:30pm,
Dinner 6pm – 9pm Thursday-Monday
Reservations: Recommended (book in advance if possible)

This is that great restaurant at Domaine Chandon winery that we talked about earlier. Étoile Restaurant touts itself as being the only fine dining restaurant inside a winery. This means they not only have a primo location, they have a great wine list. The (French influenced) menu here changes seasonally and can include beef, veal, duck and even rabbit. They have an á la carte as well as a fixed price menu.

Mustards Grill

7399 St. Helena Highway, Yountville, CA 94599 / 707-944-2424
www.mustardsgrill.com
Price: $$$
Hours: 11:30am – 9pm Monday-Thursday, 11:30am – 10pm Friday, 11am – 10pm Saturday, 11am – 9pm Sunday
Reservations: Not needed

Mustards is an American grill that grills just about anything, from steaks, fish, ribs, to you name it. They're known for their BBQ baby back ribs so be sure to sample. For dessert, you must try the lemon-lime tart with brown sugar meringue – it's fantastic.

The French Laundry

6640 Washington Street, Yountville, CA 94599 / 707-944-2380
www.frenchlaundry.com
Price: $$$$
Hours: Dinner 5:30pm – 9:15pm daily,
Lunch 11am – 1pm Friday-Sunday
Reservations: A definite must

This restaurant is the super ritzy restaurant by Chef Thomas Keller, who also runs the more casual Ad Hoc. Reservations are a must and are usually only procured way in advance. But if you dine here, you will never forget it. This restaurant has a nine course (yes, nine!) tasting menu, so you get a small taste of several delicious creations. Dinner goes for three to four hours, so it definitely is an event, though the price is pretty steep, a few hundred bucks per person. So come with plenty of time, room in your stomach and your wallet.

...tell your friends at wineopolis.com

Auberge Du Soleil

180 Rutherford Hill Road, Rutherford, CA 94573 / 800-348-5406
www.aubergedusoleil.com
Price: $$$$
Hours: Breakfast 7am – 11am daily, Lunch 11:30pm – 2:30pm Monday-Friday, Brunch 11:30am – 2:30pm Saturday-Sunday, Dinner 5:30pm – 9:30pm daily
Reservations: Required

This was first a restaurant and now it is a first class resort and restaurant. The restaurant uses as much local produce as possible, giving it a Mediterranean twist. And they have a very extensive wine list showcasing many local wineries. Best of all, there is an outdoor terrace which has stunning views of olive groves and vineyards. Be sure to sit here and take in a sunset if you can. For dinner, there is a fixed price menu with wine for around $100 per person, but lunch and other meals are á la carte. Food highlights include fresh salmon, yellowtail as well as local beef and veal.

Rutherford Grill

1180 Rutherford Road, Rutherford, CA 94573 / 707-963-1792
www.hillstone.com
Price: $$$
Hours: 11:30pm – 9:30pm Sunday-Thursday, 11:30am – 10:30pm Friday-Saturday
Reservations: Not needed

Rutherford Grill is a local chain of the larger Hillstone Restaurant Group that owns several fashionable grills in top destinations. This grill has all the basics you'd expect, like hamburgers, salads, fish and meat dishes. They have a good Caesar salad and we love the appetizer deviled eggs. But what makes this grill stand out is their wine menu, which is almost bigger than the food menu. When you want to feel relaxed and have some good American comfort food, come here. There are no reservations accepted, so be prepared to wait at dinnertime.

Go Fish

641 Main Street, St. Helena, CA 94574 / 707-963-0700
www.gofishrestaurant.net
Price: $$$$
Hours: Open daily lunch and dinner (hours vary by season so check their website)
Reservations: Recommended

Apt title for a restaurant that is known for some of the freshest fish in the region. You can ask for fish prepared "your way", meaning you decide if it's broiled, sautéed or poached, etc. There also is a very good sushi and sake bar. But

where did you go?

they don't only do fish, they also have a selection of chicken and beef – we suggest the Napa Cabernet Braised Boneless Beef Short Ribs. This is Chef Cindy Pawlcyn's third restaurant in the Napa area, (another being Mustards) and it's loved by tourists and locals alike. So come see what all the fuss is about.

Gillwoods Restaurant

1313 Main Street, St. Helena, CA 94574 / 707-963-1788
1320 Napa Town Center, Napa, CA 94559 / 707-253-0409
www.gillwoodscafe.com
Price: $$
Hours: 7am – 3pm daily (St. Helena), 7:30am – 2:30pm daily (Napa)
Reservations: Not needed

Billed as "Napa Valley home-style cooking", Gillwoods is the place you come when you love breakfast because they serve it all day, everyday...Well at least until lunch. Egg dishes abound here, the best being two eggs scrambled with smoked salmon, cream cheese and capers. But don't worry; they have lunch food, too, like burgers, sandwiches and a good Cobb salad. It's a beautifully decorated eatery with a relaxed atmosphere. And they serve wine as well, so what's not to love? They've opened a second location in Napa, so be sure to hit one on your trip.

Model Bakery

1357 Main Street, St. Helena, CA 94574 / 707-963-8192
www.themodelbakery.com
Price: $
Hours: Monday – Friday 6:30am – 5:30pm, Saturday 7am – 5:30pm, Sunday 7am – 5pm
Reservations: Not needed

We can't talk about local restaurants without listing a really great bakery. Model bakery has exquisite bagels, croissants, scones, Danishes, muffins, breads, cookies...and so on. They also have a lunch menu including fresh sandwiches, soups and brick-oven pizzas. But best of all, you can take an order to go for that winery picnic lunch we keep recommending. The bakery has been around for over eighty years and is a local favorite.

Wine Spectator Greystone Restaurant

2555 Main Street, St. Helena, CA 94574 / 707-967-1010
www.ciachef.edu
Price: $$$$
Hours: 11:30am – 9pm Sunday-Thursday, 11:30am-10pm Friday-Saturday
Reservations: Recommended

This restaurant is run by the Culinary Institute of America, but it serves as a continuing education for new chefs so you won't be eating experimentations

log it, blog it, share it at wineopolis.com

by beginners. Instead, you'll get some fresh and exciting cuisines served by future top chefs. You can expect influences from all regions. Though the menu changes frequently, you will commonly see dishes such as a petite hanger steak with bleu cheese fondue and Cabernet Sauvignon juice or red chili seafood stew. There's also a 25-page wine list, so come ready to drink some wine with your great meal.

Martini House

1245 Spring Street, St. Helena, CA 94574 / 707-963-2233
www.martinihouse.com
Price: $$$$
Hours: Open for lunch and dinner daily (hours vary by season so check their website)
Reservations: Recommended

Martini House is the blend of top Bay Area Chef Todd Humphries and renowned restaurateur Pat Kuleto (who also has a local winery). The name comes from the quaint bungalow where it is housed, once being owned by opera singer Walter Martini. The atmosphere is quaint and charming, but is second to the extensive wine list. Martini House prides itself on offering hard to find wines and the wine list itself has over 600 bottles. The restaurant also likes to use hard-to-find ingredients such as black chanterelles (mushrooms) and rosehips (berries) which they then pair with local fresh vegetables and farm-raised meats. Chef Humphries is a big lover of mushrooms and the menu abounds with creative uses of mushrooms of all kinds.

Calistoga Inn Restaurant & Brewery

1250 Lincoln Avenue, Calistoga, CA 94515 / 707-942-4101
www.calistogainn.com
Price: $$$
Hours: Daily, Lunch 11:30am – 3pm, Bar Menu 3pm – 5:30pm, Dinner 5:30pm – Closing Reservations: Not needed

The Calistoga Inn is a quaint European-style hotel that also houses a restaurant and brewery. The restaurant has patio dining overlooking the Napa River and the place is hoppin' in the summertime. The cuisine is American and the chefs cook outdoors over wood-fired grills in every season except winter. Standout dishes include the grilled pork tenderloin with fresh fruit chutney and grilled rib-eye steak with Béarnaise butter. During the summer months the restaurant has live jazz music on the patio during dinner and the brewery next door is always a fun night spot whatever the season.

bite, munch, blog, repeat

All Seasons Café

1400 Lincoln Avenue, Calistoga, CA 94515 / 707-942-9111
www.allseasonsnapavalley.net
Price: $$$$
Hours: Daily for lunch and dinner (check website for specifics)
Reservations: Not needed

All Seasons Café is your uber-healthy choice. They pride themselves on using organic and chemical-free produce, meats and poultry. The majority of their items come from local producers, so they are also doing their part to support the local economy. The cuisine is American and though the menu changes daily, you can always count on having a variety of meats and fresh fish to choose from. They also have a lot of local wines, as well as standout wines from across the globe.

Calistoga Roastery

1426 Lincoln Avenue, Calistoga, CA 94515 / 707-942-5757
www.calistogaroastery.com
Price: $
Hours: Daily 6:30am – 6pm
Reservations: None

With all this talk about wine, it's nice to know there are some other options when you need a respite. This local gem produces a great cup of coffee; so much so, that most local restaurants serve it. There's also a café, so you can come for breakfast or lunch and have a wide selection of scones, muffins, sandwiches, salads and fruit smoothies. But we're really a sucker for a great cup of Joe, and this is the place. So forgo a coffee chain and come sit for a while in this quaint yet comfortable coffee shop.

Wappo Bar & Bistro

1226 Washington Street, Calistoga, CA 94515 / 707-942-4712
www.wappobar.com
Price: $$$
Hours: Lunch 11:30am – 2:30pm, Dinner 6pm – 9pm Wednesday-Monday (closed Tuesday)
Reservations: Recommended

This restaurant is off the main drag in Calistoga, but it is well worth finding. This local eatery is relaxed and casual, with copper-topped tables, a redwood wine bar and outdoor brick patio surrounded by trees. If you're looking for a peaceful meal, then this is the place. The menu has influences from all across the globe and is great for both lunch and dinner. Favorite dishes include the Brazilian seafood chowder, halibut with Thai green curry and the Wappo chiles rellenos with walnut pomegranate sauce.

post your trip photos at wineopolis.com

Trip Log: Places to Eat

Restaurant: _____

Town: _____

Meal: Dinner   Lunch   Breakfast   Other

_____

Price: _____

What did you eat? _____

What did you like about it? _____

Notes: _____

_____

_____

_____

_____

_____

_____

_____

_____

_____

Rating

1	2	3	4	5
Don't Like It		It's Okay		I Love It!

find free resources at wineopolis.com

Trip Log: Places to Eat

Restaurant: _____

Town: _____

Meal: Dinner   Lunch   Breakfast   Other

_____

Price: _____

What did you eat? _____

What did you like about it? _____

Notes: _____

_____

_____

_____

_____

_____

_____

_____

_____

_____

_____

_____

Rating

1	2	3	4	5
Don't Like It		It's Okay		I Love It!

Share your experiences online at wineopolis.com

Trip Log: Places to Eat

Restaurant: _____

Town: _____

Meal: Dinner   Lunch   Breakfast   Other

_____

Price: _____

What did you eat? _____

What did you like about it? _____

Notes: _____

_____

_____

_____

_____

_____

_____

_____

_____

_____

Rating

1	2	3	4	5
Don't Like It		It's Okay		I Love It!

let us know your favorites at wineopolis.com

Trip Log: Places to Eat

Restaurant: _____

Town: _____

Meal: Dinner   Lunch   Breakfast   Other
                    _____

Price: _____

What did you eat? _____

What did you like about it? _____

Notes: _____
_____
_____
_____
_____
_____
_____
_____
_____
_____
_____
_____

Rating

1	2	3	4	5
Don't Like It		It's Okay		I Love It!

Share your experiences online at wineopolis.com

Napa Activities Not to be Missed

Okay, so we know you can't taste wine *all* the time, even though it's mainly why you come here. But, there are some great attractions in Napa that you really should make the time to see and do. If you can peel yourself away from the tasting table, they're well worth a few hours. We will again go geographically, starting in the south and take you through the best sights, shops and events you need to see.

But what really makes Wineopolis.com so effective is our shared knowledge and experiences, so don't forget to record your travels and come share them with the rest of us at Wineopolis.com.

Napa Valley Wine Train

1275 McKinstry Street, Napa, CA / 800-427-4124
www.winetrain.com
Price: $50-100 per person

The wine train is actually a moving restaurant that provides a luxury experience while you take in the scenery. This bright mahogany, gold and green passenger train moves at a leisurely pace from Napa to St. Helena and then back again. Taking a bit of inspiration from the old Orient Express, the interior boasts mahogany paneling, crystal chandeliers and plush seats that swivel so you can take in the view. As you move across the landscape, you'll pass towns, wineries and vineyards as far as the eye can see. The whole excursion is three to four hours and the price depends on whether you travel for brunch, lunch, dinner or the bi-monthly Murder Mystery tour. All meals come with a selection of still and sparkling wines, of course. The train takes off from downtown Napa and reservations are a must.

Balloons Above The Valley

Office: 603 California Blvd., Napa, CA 94559 / 800-464-6824
www.balloonrides.com
Take-off: 540 Main Street, Napa, CA 94559
Price: $230 per person (but they always have specials, so check the website)

This is the premier hot-air balloon company in Napa and they provide a unique way to see all of Napa Valley – from the air. These hot-air balloon rides will take you above the trees and glide you gently over countless wineries and vineyards. Balloons Above the Valley will pick you up from your hotel, take you up in the air for about an hour and even serve a champagne brunch. These rides go fast, so be sure to call ahead for a reservation.

make notes in your Trip Log at the end of this section

Oxbow Public Market

610 & 644 First Street, Downtown Napa, CA 94559
www.oxbowpublicmarket.com
Hours: Open daily (hours depend on shops, usually 9am – 7pm)

The Oxbow Public Market is a larger conglomeration of food and wine purveyors, restaurants and retail shops – all under one big roof. It's like a big specialty food mall. Here you will find specialty vendors offering exclusive gourmet foods, wines, cheeses, gifts, knick-knacks and souvenirs of all types. It's a great venue for local food producers and it also gives you a chance to support local growers and wineries. They usually have lots of events happening here, such as live music and festivals, so check the events section of their website.

Napa Valley Opera House

1030 Main Street Napa, CA 94559 / 707-226-7372
www.nvoh.org
Price: Varies

The Napa Valley Opera House is the best place in all of Napa County for live music, jazz, opera and musical theater. This establishment was first opened 130 years ago, though it had a complete renovation by Robert Mondavi and reopened in 2002 after many decades of dormancy. Still, it's definitely a cultural icon not to be missed. Even if you don't see a show here, it's worth a visit to check out the long history of the building and marvel in its grandeur. Check the website for upcoming shows and events.

Seguin Moreau Napa Cooperage

151 Camino Dorado, Napa, CA 94559 / 707-252-3408
www.seguin-moreau.fr
Price: Free
Hours: 9:30am – 12:30 pm Monday-Friday
(self tours)

This is the only U.S. location of the French company that specializes in making wine-barrels. The process has been used for ages and is fun to watch. From bending the wood, to "toasting" it over open flames in the floor, then hammering the pieces together and applying the steel hoops, it provides you, the observer, the chance to see how it's been done for hundreds of years. It's free to observe and you can also take a self-guided tour Monday through Friday mornings.

Share your experiences online at wineopolis.com

Napa Valley & Sonoma Bike Tours

6488 Washington Street, Yountville, CA 94599 / 800-707-2453
www.napavalleybiketours.com
Price: $139 per person for tour, $25-75 for bike rental depending on bike and time

If you plan on tasting a lot of wine and food, working some of those calories off on a bike may be the way to go in beautiful Wine Country. Biking your way around Wine Country is very popular, not to mention very fun. But don't head out alone. If you're unsure of the landscape, you might want to bike and tour with others. The Napa Valley & Sonoma Bike Tours offers winery tours that begin at 9:30am and end at 3pm. Not only do you get your own bike and helmet, you will enjoy a catered picnic as well as the knowledge of a local guide. You won't need to worry about getting wine home; they have a van where you can have your bottles sent back to the main location. If you don't want to do a tour, they also rent bikes for either two hours or for the entire day. Tandem bikes are available.

Napa Valley Museum

55 Presidents Circle, Yountville, CA 94599 / 707-944-0500
www.napavalleymuseum.com
Hours: 10am - 5pm Wednesday - Monday
Price: $4.50 adults, children 12 and under are free

This non-profit museum was built to honor the historical and cultural heritage of the surrounding Napa Valley. There is a permanent exhibit called "The Land and People of the Napa Valley" which explores the history of the region as well as the winemaking process. There are other rotating exhibits covering topics from fine arts to natural sciences. Check the website to see what's currently on exhibition.

Lincoln Theater

100 California Drive, Yountville, CA 94599 / 707-944-1300
www.lincolntheater.com
Price: Varies

The Lincoln Theater has also had a major renovation of late and re-opened with much fanfare in 2005. This theater is home to the Napa Symphony and boasts a 1,200 seat theater including a balcony. Despite the Symphony, the theatre has quite a diverse musical lineup as well as speakers, shows and comedians. The theatre lies on the same grounds as the California Veterans Home, a community for and by veterans. Check the website for information, shows and tickets.

what else did you do?

Silverado Museum

1490 Library Lane, St. Helena, CA 94574 / 707-963-3757
www.silveradomuseum.org
Hours: 12pm – 4pm Wednesday-Sunday
Price: Free

This museum is dedicated to author Robert Lewis Stevenson (1850-1894). You may know the name from such books as Treasure Island and Dr. Jekyll and Mr. Hyde. But he also wrote The Silverado Squatters which accounts Stevenson's stay in an abandoned bunkhouse in nearby Silverado Mine back in 1888. This museum houses many Stevenson memorabilia, mostly collected by a local man named Norman H. Strauss. The museum has first edition prints of some of Stevenson books, as well as handwritten letters and photographs. A great place to research and learn about this well-known and loved author.

Dean & Deluca

607 St. Helena Highway S., St. Helena, CA 94574 / 707-967-9980
www.deandeluca.com
Hours: 7am – 7pm Sunday-Thursday, 7am – 8pm Friday-Saturday

If you're looking for a grocery store that also delivers a great experience, then don't miss out on Dean & Deluca. First started on the east coast, the Napa location of this premium store prides itself on gourmet foods, an enormous California wine selection, fancy kitchenware, fresh local produce, local artisan cheeses, a deli, bakery and espresso bar. It's a lot to pack into one space, but Dean & Deluca does it in style. If you're looking for somewhere to fill up your picnic basket, come here.

Culinary Institute Of America At Greystone

2555 Main Street, St. Helena, CA 94574 / 888-424-2433
www.ciastore.com
Price: Free (Cooking demonstrations are $15 per person)

The Culinary Institute is a premier school for aspiring chefs, but visiting here is also a treat. For starters, there's the upscale eatery, Wine Spectator Restaurant, we've already told you about. If you're not in the mood to eat fancy, there's a small café with pastries and breads cooked by students that is open daily. But best of all, there's the Spice Islands Marketplace which is a chef superstore. Here you can find an assortment of cookbooks, cooking utensils, gadgets, pots, pans, and equipment. You name it, they have it. The institute also holds cooking demonstrations, where for $15 you can learn and then taste afterwards. You'll need to check the website for times and call for reservations. However, it's free to roam the Institute. It's in an enormous,

...tell your friends at wineopolis.com

ancient-looking stone building, so you cannot miss it and the building used to occupy the former Christian Brothers winery before it was changed to a culinary campus in the 1990s.

Art On Main

1359 Main Street, St. Helena, CA 94574 / 707-963-3350
www.imagesnapavalley.com
Price: Free
Hours: 10am – 5:30pm daily

This art gallery places a focus on images of vineyards and wine. It's why you came here, right? So venture in to take in the artistic interpretations by many local artists. You can see original oil paintings, watercolors, acrylic and even mixed media artwork. The gallery is open daily and will add a taste of local culture to your trip.

Bale Grist Mill State Historic Park

3369 Highway 29, St. Helena, CA 94574 / 707-942-4575
www.parks.ca.gov/?page_id=482
Price: $2 for adults, children under 16 are free
Hours: 10am – 5pm Saturday-Sunday

Located three miles north of St. Helena is this historic park which centers around a water-powered grist mill erected back in 1846. It was here that settlers would have their wheat and corn ground into flour. Besides taking a tour of the facility, which includes the area's first church and cemetery, you can also hike on a historic trail leading up to Bothe – Napa Valley State Park. It's open on weekends, but be sure to check the website for updates on closures.

St. Helena Olive Oil Co.

8576 Highway 29, Napa, CA 94558 / 707-967-1003 ext.14
1351 Main Street, St. Helena, CA 94574 / 800-939-9880
www.sholiveoil.com
Hours: 10:30am – 5pm daily

Though you may come to Napa with wine on the brain, olive oil is also a standout product made locally. Olive oil is a taste-bud luxury and at this store it gets the royal treatment. Not only does this store have some of the best olive oil you can buy, you get to taste them, too. They also make some of their own balsamic vinegar, including a popular Cabernet vinegar. So while enjoying some of the best wine, breads and cheeses made locally, add some local olive oil and balsamic to the mix.

what did you see?

Woodhouse Chocolate

1367 Main Street, St. Helena, CA 94574 / 800-966-3468
www.woodhousechocolate.com
Hours: 10:30am – 5:30pm daily

You're in Napa for a little luxury, so don't forgo another great luxury – chocolate. This store has some exquisite gourmet chocolates and they're all made in the kitchen right behind the main salon by the owners, the Anderson family. Get ready to be wowed by the many display cases filled with delectable chocolate treats instead of jewels. The owners pride themselves on using only the best nuts, creams, butters and spices they can find. You will definitely want to pick up a few to take with you wherever you go.

Bothe-Napa Valley State Park

Highway 29, south of Calistoga / 707-942-4575
www.parks.ca.gov/default.asp?page_id=477
Price: $6 per car
Hours: 8am – sunset daily

This park is great for all those wine and lunch picnics you'll want to take. Just off of Highway 29 is this expansive park, which has several varieties of trees from coastal redwoods, Douglas fir, tanoak and madrone – perfect for an afternoon rest or an invigorating hike. The park has camping, swimming, hiking, and plenty of locations for that picnic. The park also offers guided horse rides (for a fee). Check the website for any updates, closures or advisories.

The Sharpsteen Museum

1311 Washington Street, Calistoga, CA 94515 / 707-942-5911
www.sharpsteen-museum.org
Price: $3 for adults, children under 12 are free
Hours: 11am – 4pm daily

This museum is named after founder Ben Sharpsteen, who was an animator, director and producer on many iconic films for Walt Disney such as Snow White. In fact, you can even see his Oscar he won during his time with Disney on display. Inside, however, is a history of the region. The museum tells the tale of the northern Napa Valley from the early days to post World War I. Abutting the museum is a restored white cottage from an early hot springs resort by Sam Brannan ('California's first millionaire') in the 1860s. Though, if you look close you'll swear it was plucked straight from Disneyland. It's a pleasant museum chock full of interesting history about the region.

post your trip photos at wineopolis.com

American Indian Trading Company

1407 Lincoln Avenue, Calistoga, CA 94515 / 707-942-9330
www.aitcoc.com
Hours: 10am – 6pm daily

This store is considered an "undiscovered gem" and we couldn't agree more. The American Indian Trading Company is jam packed with Native American culture. If you love jewelry, then you have your pick of turquoise, as well as opal and amber. You can also find many other handcrafted artifacts, be it pots, flutes, moccasins or sculptures that make great souvenirs or gifts. Make sure to drop in. You're likely to find something special.

Villa Ca'toga / Ca'toga Galleria D'arte

House: Calistoga, CA 94515 / 707-942-3900
www.catoga.com
Gallery: 1206 Cedar Street, CA 94515
www.catoga.com/galleria
Price: $25 per person (House)
Hours: House: Saturday 11am (May – October only) /
Gallery: 11am – 6pm Thursday-Monday

Ca'Toga (the house) is a sight to behold, in a unique and artistic way. It's actually a house, modeled after an Italian villa, by Italian artist Carlo Marchiori. It's still a work in progress, but you won't believe your eyes when you step inside this mansion. Carlo Marchiori is a muralist who specializes in period art and he can reproduce Renaissance, Baroque and Neoclassic styles perfectly. So he's turned his house into a big, sprawling mural. There are faux staircases, pillars, gardens and life-size statues which all look so real, you'll do a double-take when you see they are murals. It's like going to a live art museum and we highly recommend it if you are in the area. The house is only open for a one-hour tour on Saturdays from May to October for $25. If you'd like to see his murals in a proper gallery setting, then visit the Ca'Toga Galleria D'Arte on Cedar Street. It's open Thursday through Monday year-round.

Calistoga Pottery

1001 Foothill Boulevard, Calistoga, CA 94515 / 707-942-0216
www.calistogapottery.com
Hours: 11am – 5pm daily

Local pottery from local artists, that's what you'll find at Calistoga Pottery. Owners Sally and Jeff Manfredi make everything in the pottery studio out of their own home. You'll find durable yet artistic stoneware in everything from platters and plates, to pitchers, bowls and coffee mugs. They do a lot

play, shop, blog, repeat

of "made to order" work, but there is a selection of past works for sale on the shelves where you're sure to find a one-of-a-kind souvenir. The gallery also has a selection of favorite works on display, so it's worth a browse at the very least.

Petrified Forest

4100 Petrified Forest Road, Calistoga, CA 94515 / 707-942-6667
www.petrifiedforest.org
Price: $8 for adults, $6 for children 12-17, and seniors over 60, $3 for children 6-11
Hours: 9am – 7pm daily (store and museum) - closes at 5pm in winter

A petrified forest allows you to see history in a freeze frame. Massive volcano eruptions once coated this northern part of the valley in ash. Thankfully, this was millions of years ago and the volcano is now dormant, but you can still see the hardened ash and petrified redwood trees that are forever preserved. The highlight is a giant redwood called Monarch that is 105 feet tall with a diameter of six feet. But, there are several other trails through the area, all offering many petrified sights. There is a store and museum on-site so you can learn more and buy related merchandise.

Share your experiences online at wineopolis.com

Trip Log: Things to See & Do

Name: _____

Town: _____

Category: Recreation   Shopping   Museum   Music   Culture   Family

Price: _____

What did you like about it? _____

_____

Notes: _____

_____

_____

_____

_____

_____

_____

_____

_____

_____

Rating

1	2	3	4	5
Don't Like It		It's Okay		I Love It!

log it, blog it, share it at wineopolis.com

Trip Log: Things to See & Do

Name: _____

Town: _____

Category: Recreation   Shopping   Museum   Music   Culture   Family

Price: _____

What did you like about it? _____

_____

Notes: _____

_____
_____
_____
_____
_____
_____
_____
_____
_____
_____
_____

Rating

1	2	3	4	5
Don't Like It		It's Okay		I Love It!

let us know your favorites at wineopolis.com

Trip Log: Things to See & Do

Name: _____

Town: _____

Category: Recreation   Shopping   Museum   Music   Culture   Family

Price: _____

What did you like about it? _____

_____

Notes: _____

_____
_____
_____
_____
_____
_____
_____
_____
_____
_____
_____

Rating

1	2	3	4	5
Don't Like It		It's Okay		I Love It!

let us know your favorites at wineopolis.com

Trip Log: Things to See & Do

Name: _____

Town: _____

Category: Recreation   Shopping   Museum   Music   Culture   Family

Price: _____

What did you like about it? _____

_____

Notes: _____

_____
_____
_____
_____
_____
_____
_____
_____
_____
_____
_____
_____

Rating

1	2	3	4	5
Don't Like It		It's Okay		I Love It!

Share your experiences online at wineopolis.com

Where to Stay in Napa

Finally we've come to the part where we list all the fabulous places you can stay during your trip! Where you sleep is as much a part of the experience as where you sip. So in the following pages, we outline some of our favorites. We'll cover a variety so as to fit all tastes, including hotels, motels, resorts, and bed & breakfasts. We'll list the chains you know, as well as some local gems. For us, comfort is king, as you need to be well rested to enjoy all that wine tasting. And, if you choose to stay somewhere else and have a fabulous time, come share your experience with us at Wineopolis.com! We're always looking for new and exciting places.

Again, we will start our list with Napa and work our way north up the valley. We'll list the name, address and contact information, price, location, as well as a description of the amenities you can expect.

Note on prices: Hotel rates vary by season and occasion, so we have provided a price range according to their listed regular rates during the high season months. It is best to always check the hotel website for your specific dates to see what rates and specials apply.

PRICE GUIDE (per night based on double occupancy):

$ - Less than $100
$$ - $101 to $175
$$$ - $176 to $250
$$$$ - More than $251

Gaia Napa Valley Hotel & Spa

3600 Broadway St., American Canyon, CA 94503 / 888-798-3777
www.gaiahotelnapavalley.com
Price: $$

This is the hotel for those of you wanting to travel green, as their motto is "Affordable. Sustainable. Luxurious." That sure is music to our ears. The name Gaia means "mother Earth" in Greek, so you can expect them to deliver a natural and relaxing environment. The rooms are simple, impeccable and comfortable. There's also a full service spa and restaurant. Located just south of Napa, this hotel is a short drive to most of your winery destinations, and it serves as a great compromise between luxury and affordability.

make notes in your Trip Log at the end of this section

River Terrace Inn

1600 Soscol Avenue, Napa, CA 94558 / 866-627-2386
www.riverterraceinn.com
Price: $$$$

This Inn, located in the hotspot of downtown Napa, offers mostly suites with balconies where you can take in the view of the Napa River and valley. They tout themselves as a boutique luxury hotel and they aren't lying. The rooms are warm and elegant, and most have a spectacular view. There is a private spa, outdoor pool, fitness center and complimentary buffet breakfast. The Terrace Café offers salads and sandwiches at lunch, as well as dinner. But our favorite is the on-site wine bar which offers many wines from local wineries.

Churchill Manor Bed & Breakfast Inn

485 Brown Street, Napa, CA 94588 / 800-799-7733
www.churchillmanor.com
Price: $$$$

This three-story mansion was first built for Edward Churchill, a local Napa banker, back in 1889. It has been meticulously maintained. For many years, this was the largest house around and its grandeur is only matched by its elegance. The inside boasts not one but four parlor rooms, all furnished with leaded glass, redwood moldings and large fireplaces. The rooms themselves are reminiscent of an English countryside manor. There is a full breakfast each morning, as well as afternoon wine, cheese and cookies. Just wandering the house or the acre of luscious gardens is well worth the price. This is also a prime wedding location if you're in the market.

La Belle Epoque

1386 Calistoga Avenue, Napa, CA 94558 / 800-238-8070
www.labelleepoque.com
Price: $$$ - $$$$

La Belle Époque is French for "the beautiful era" and usually refers to a time of renaissance in France from 1871 – 1914. This charming building, which boasts an ornate Queen Anne style, was built in 1893 by a local hardware dealer. Now, it serves as a charming B&B in the midst of Napa. It has nine rooms (each lavishly decorated) and an outdoor Victorian garden. There is a full complimentary breakfast, but what gets us excited is their nightly wine reception. La Belle Époque has its own on-site wine cellar, which they open up in the evenings for guests to sip some great local wines while enjoying complimentary appetizers.

Share your experiences online at wineopolis.com

Travelodge

853 Coombs Street, Napa, CA 94558 / 866-520-5948
www.travelodge.com
Price: $$

This hotel is on our list mostly for its location. In the heart of downtown Napa, this hotel has you steps away from all the action. Restaurants, shops and the Wine Train depot are all nearby. This Travelodge is as nice as they come, having been recently renovated. The rooms are neat and comfortable. There's a complimentary breakfast and you can't beat the price. A great choice if you plan on spending most of your time out and about.

Inn On Randolph

411 Randolph Street, Napa, CA 94588 / 800-670-6886
www.innonrandolph.com
Price: $$$

This charming B&B is located on a residential street lined with historic homes - most Victorian. The Inn on Randolph is itself an 1860 Victorian home, with attached cottages, making it a home away from home (though a very nice one). Each room and cottage has its own theme; our favorites are the Spring and Autumn rooms in the main house. The adjoining cottages all have fireplaces as well as tubs built for two. You can enjoy a full breakfast every morning and even order an in-room massage. Community areas include a club lounge, spa lounge, game room, sun room and dining salon. This property is well suited for a romantic getaway or business retreat.

The John Muir Inn

1998 Trower Avenue, Napa, CA 94558 / 800-522-8999
www.johnmuirnapa.com
Price: $$

Taking inspiration from famed naturalist John Muir, who was such an influence to preserving the land around the Sierra Nevada range in California, this is a simple and modest hotel. The location in Napa is its greatest advantage, as it really is the gateway to a whole host of wineries and sights. There is a free continental breakfast, as well as an outdoor courtyard with pool and whirlpool. Most of the rooms have kitchenettes (perfect for all that food and wine you've been collecting) and the front desk is very knowledgeable about the area.

where did you stay?

Napa Valley Marriott Hotel & Spa

3425 Solano Avenue, Napa, CA 94558 / 800-228-9290
www.napavalleymarriott.com
Price: $$$

The Napa Valley Marriott offers everything you can expect from a large hotel. It has upwards of 270 rooms as well as an on-site spa, fitness center, heated outdoor pool and whirlpool, laundry service, gift shop, as well as complimentary parking. Speaking of complimentary services, this hotel has a daily complimentary wine tasting from various wineries. Harvest Café is the hotel restaurant and it has a delectable selection of California cuisine. It is located just off Highway 29 in Napa itself.

Milliken Creek Inn And Spa

1815 Silverado Trail, Napa, CA 94558 / 800-835-6112
www.millikencreekinn.com
Price: $$$$

This elegant Inn sits on three acres overlooking the Napa River as you head toward the populated Wine Country off Napa's famous Silverado Trail. The Inn itself is somewhat romantic, priding itself on complete pampering of their guests. Rooms here have luxury beds, fireplaces and oversized tubs perfect for a relaxing soak. Your stay will include a gourmet breakfast, served in your room or on their terrace, as well as a sunset wine and cheese tasting. There is a spa on location featuring holistic and therapeutic treatments. You'll have plenty of privacy (there's only 12 guestrooms) to take in the peace and quiet of the Napa countryside. It's the perfect Inn for those truly looking to "get away from it all", though pricey, with most rooms going upwards of $500.

Brookside Vineyard Bed & Breakfast

3194 Redwood Road, Napa, CA / 707-252-6690
www.sandtcellars.com
Price: $$$

Brookside is not only a bed & breakfast; it's also a working vineyard, bottling a Petite Syrah for Sand T Cellars. There are only three guestrooms and they are housed in a charming Mediterranean style inn at the top of an idyllic tree lined lane. The common rooms of the house are tastefully decorated with a mixture of hand crafted furniture and antiques. There is a full gourmet breakfast that is served in a gazebo overlooking the pool and garden during the summer months. Complimentary wine is served in the afternoons, either inside or out. This B&B is a great way to see first-hand, the goings-on of a working vineyard, while still enjoying a nice retreat.

...tell your friends at wineopolis.com

Maison Fleurie

6529 Yount Street, Yountville, CA 94599 / 800-788-0369
www.maisonfleurienapa.com
Price: $$$ - $$$$

The Maison Fleurie (French for "flowering house") was built to evoke the charm of the southern French countryside. The main building is over 100 years old and made of stone. Covered with twisting vines, this flowering house is so beautiful, it looks like it belongs in a painting. You can expect a lot of bright colors, floral prints, and plenty of French toile in their 13 rooms. There is a full breakfast every morning, as well as afternoon wine, tea and hors d'oeuvres, and there are always fresh-baked cookies available. This B&B is part of the Four Sisters Inns chain, which is known for some stellar locations throughout California.

Napa Valley Railway Inn

6523 Washington Street, Yountville, CA 94599 / 707-944-2000
www.napavalleyrailwayinn.com
Price: $$$

If you're looking to stay somewhere unique, then look no further than the Napa Valley Railway Inn. This hotel is housed in 100-year old train cars on an actual old railway track, that have been converted into accommodations. The building still looks like a train car from the days of old. The nine rooms are all rather atypically sized, but they are beautifully appointed with each room having its own distinct character. But they all have queen or king-sized beds, a bath and sitting area. There is a fitness center nearby which is complimentary for all guests. Even better, this Inn is within walking distance from all of the Yountville restaurants and shops you'll want to visit.

Bordeaux House

6600 Washington Street, Yountville, CA 94599 / 800-677-6370
www.bordeauxhouse.com
Price: $$$$

Bordeaux House is located in the middle of Yountville and the property has a mix of old buildings (circa late 1800s) and newer ones (circa late 1900s). The red brick buildings have both English and French influences; as do the surrounding gardens. There are eight guest rooms, most named after different wine varietals, and a charming reception area complete with a large fireplace. They offer a hot and cold buffet breakfast which you can enjoy in your room if you wish. There's also an outdoor whirlpool. The Bordeaux House offers significantly lower room rates in the off season (winter), when there are fewer crowds.

sleep, shower, blog, repeat

Rancho Caymus Inn

1140 Rutherford Cross Road, Rutherford, CA 94573 / 800-845-1777
www.ranchocaymus.com
Price: $$$$

The Rancho Caymus Inn pays homage to the Spanish missions of old and it does so in style. It's nestled along a row of wineries and is a great escape for those looking to stay off the beaten path. The white stucco walls, tiled roof and aged beams are very picturesque, making this Inn a popular place for weddings and special events. Inside the furnishings are all original pieces hailing from many South American regions, giving the room an old-world feel while still being luxurious. The Inn wraps around a beautiful garden courtyard where you can take in the beauty of nature. A continental breakfast is included with your stay as well.

El Bonita Motel

195 Main Street, St. Helena, CA 94574 / 800-541-3284
www.elbonita.com
Price: $ - $$

The El Bonita Motel is a throwback to the 1950s - just take a look at the bright neon sign with a flickering "Vacancy" beckoning you in. It's a motel, to be sure, and an eclectic one. Each room is slightly different, though all furnishings are far from modern. There's a continental breakfast, fireplace in the lobby, outdoor pool with Jacuzzi and patio for eating or relaxing. There's nothing standout about this place, but it's in a great central location in St. Helena, and the rooms are comfortable and clean.

The Wine Country Inn & Gardens

1152 Lodi Lane, St. Helena, CA 94574 / 888-465-4608
www.winecountryinn.com
Price: $$$$

This Inn has a decidedly country feel, with its remote location, small size, and down-home furnishings. There are a combination of rooms, suites and private cottages, and almost all have a balcony with a stunning view of the surrounding landscape (which includes a vineyard). But what makes this Inn stand out are all of the complimentary services for guests: full buffet breakfast, afternoon food and wine, and shuttle to nearby restaurants. This Inn is the perfect romantic getaway for honeymooners and couples looking to renew that spark (there's no television in any of the rooms). If you have a family, then you might want to look at some other places to stay.

Share your experiences online at wineopolis.com

Hotel St. Helena

1309 Main Street, St. Helena, CA 94574 / 888-478-4355
www.hotelsthelena.net
Price: $$$ - $$$$

For those looking to stay close to the action (what action there is in Wine Country), this hotel is conveniently located in downtown St. Helena. The hotel was originally built in 1881 as a premier luxury hotel, though it fell into disrepair soon after. But thankfully, it has been completely restored and is now the epitome of luxury. On the first floor are many boutique shops and with the rooms upstairs. There are only 17 rooms (plus one suite), but they are richly decorated in hues of gold, burgundy and chocolate brown – a true Victorian treat. There is a complimentary breakfast, as well as complimentary wine in the afternoons. This hotel is pricey, but they offer discounts if you stay here mid-week, so look to come here on off-days maybe during the less popular seasons.

Shady Oaks Country Inn

399 Zinfandel Lane, St. Helena, CA 94574 / 707-963-11901
www.shadyoakscountryinn.com
Price: $$$$

This bed & breakfast is on two acres of land, comprised of a walnut orchard and vineyard. There are only five rooms in two buildings, making this a very private lodging choice. The first building contains two suites in what was once an old stone winery built in the late 1880s. Next door is a craftsman-style home built in the 1920s that houses three more rooms. All rooms are filled with charming antiques and decorative furniture. Not only do they have a full breakfast, it's a champagne breakfast. That's how we like to start our day! There's also complimentary wine and cheese in the evening.

Glass Mountain Inn

3100 Silverado Trail, St. Helena, CA 94574 / 877-968-9400
www.glassmountaininn.com
Price: $$$$

This bed & breakfast is up in the mountains outside of St. Helena, making it a perfect hideaway. Glass Mountain Inn is family owned and sits on two acres, yet it is still close to local restaurants and shops. They use locally-grown products when they can and have many organic food items, including a great cup of organic coffee. The name of the Inn comes from the abundance of obsidian glass that is found in the area and it is used in some of the interior decor. There are five rooms, including a private cottage and a two-bedroom suite. All rooms come with bathrobes as well as wine glasses, corkscrew and ice bucket. From the dining room, you can enter a wine cave which was built by Chinese laborers back in the late 1800s.

log it, blog it, share it at wineopolis.com

Clarion Collection Lodge At Calistoga

1865 Lincoln Avenue, Calistoga, CA 94515 / 877-424-6423
www.clarionhotel.com
Price: $$$$

This hotel from the Clarion chain is one of only a few in the area to utilize the many natural springs that are abundant in Calistoga by using an underground hot spring to fill and heat the hotel's outdoor pool and hot tub. The Lodge is also partnered with a local spa just minutes down the road and the services can be billed to your room. There's a free continental breakfast, fitness center, as well as a sauna and steam room. Another added bonus is that all rooms have refrigerators.

Mount View Hotel & Spa

1457 Lincoln Avenue, Calistoga, CA 94515 / 800-816-6877
www.mountviewhotel.com
Price: $$$$

At the Mount View Hotel & Spa the theme is creativity. The hotel likes to foster the idea of art, whether in regards to wine or relaxation. You can even check out an easel loaded with paints so you can try your hand at painting the inspiration that the local gardens provide. The hotel has a spacious lobby that leads to either the hotel or an adjoining spa (Mount View Spa). They have a mixture of rooms, suites and cottages all ornately furnished. There's a complimentary breakfast, like most places, but here it's delivered right to your room. This hotel has a long history with many notable figures from America and beyond having stayed here over the years. So take an opportunity to experience what they did - luxuriating in the heart of Wine Country.

Calistoga Inn

1250 Lincoln Avenue, Calistoga, CA 94515 / 707-942-4101
www.calistogainn.com
Price: $

When you walk into the Calistoga Inn, you feel like you're stepping into the Old West. Which isn't far off, as this hotel dates back to 1882. If you're looking for a full-scale resort with all the frills, this is probably not the place to be, but if you're coming to Napa for something new, then you won't forget your stay here. This hotel pays homage to hotels from the turn of the century, so modern design is not their forte. The floors might creak with history and the rooms are small (beds are no bigger than queen size) with shared bathrooms but we like it because it's charming and it fosters a social atmosphere. There's a restaurant on-site, as well as a microbrewery and bar which are worth the visit. (Highlighted in our Restaurant section).

what did you see?

The Pink Mansion

1415 Foothill Boulevard, Calistoga, CA 94515 / 800-238-7465
www.pinkmansion.com
Price: $$$$

If you want to live in the lap of luxury, then look no further than The Pink Mansion. This B&B is an eclectic mix of Victorian and Asian design, mostly due to previous owner Alma Simic. Inside there is a large parlor, complete with stunning crystal chandeliers. The building was first built in the 1870s by William F. Fisher who was an early pioneer in Calistoga. It is located in the city, a short walk from shops and restaurants. But the real draw is the décor. The seven rooms all have private baths, flat screen TVs and plush robes. Rates include a gourmet breakfast as well as afternoon wine and hors d'oeuvres. There's also an indoor heated pool and Jacuzzi. A truly stunning mansion.

Wine Way Inn

1019 Foothill Boulevard, Calistoga, CA 94515 / 800-572-0679
www.winewayinn.com
Price: $$ - $$$

If you're looking for a charming B&B that's not exorbitantly priced, then check out the Wine Way Inn. This was, in fact, the first B&B in Calistoga, though now it's near a busy intersection. But, noise aside, this is a very quaint home done in the craftsman style of the early 1900s. There are a total of 6 rooms; one of them is detached - The Calistoga Room. They serve a gourmet breakfast in the morning and complimentary wine in the evening. When you want a central location yet the feel of a bed & breakfast, this place is the perfect blend.

post your trip photos at wineopolis.com

Trip Log: Places to Stay

Name: _____

Town: _____

Type: Hotel   Motel   Resort   B&B

_____

Price: _____

What amenities did they have? _____

_____

Spa   Breakfast   Dining   Internet/WiFi   Room Service   Pool/Jacuzzi   Parking

What did you like about it? _____

_____

Notes: _____

_____
_____
_____
_____
_____
_____
_____
_____
_____
_____

Rating

1	2	3	4	5
Don't Like It		It's Okay		I Love It!

Share your experiences online at wineopolis.com

Trip Log: Places to Stay

Name: _____

Town: _____

Type: Hotel   Motel   Resort   B&B

_____

Price: _____

What amenities did they have? _____

_____

Spa   Breakfast   Dining   Internet/WiFi   Room Service   Pool/Jacuzzi   Parking

What did you like about it? _____

_____

Notes: _____

_____
_____
_____
_____
_____
_____
_____
_____
_____
_____
_____
_____

Rating

1	2	3	4	5
Don't Like It		It's Okay		I Love It!

Share your experiences online at wineopolis.com

Trip Log: Places to Stay

Name: _____

Town: _____

Type: Hotel   Motel   Resort   B&B

_____

Price: _____

What amenities did they have? _____

_____

Spa   Breakfast   Dining   Internet/WiFi   Room Service   Pool/Jacuzzi   Parking

What did you like about it? _____

_____

Notes: _____

_____
_____
_____
_____
_____
_____
_____
_____
_____
_____
_____

Rating

1	2	3	4	5
Don't Like It		It's Okay		I Love It!

Share your experiences online at wineopolis.com

Trip Log: Places to Stay

Name: _____

Town: _____

Type: Hotel Motel Resort B&B

_____

Price: _____

What amenities did they have? _____

_____

Spa Breakfast Dining Internet/WiFi Room Service Pool/Jacuzzi Parking

What did you like about it? _____

_____

Notes: _____

_____
_____
_____
_____
_____
_____
_____
_____
_____
_____
_____

Rating

1	2	3	4	5
Don't Like It		It's Okay		I Love It!

Share your experiences online at wineopolis.com

SHARE YOUR JOURNEY!

Keep in mind that the members of Wineopolis are gathered together to learn from each other's experiences. Keep track of your tasting notes, reviews, excursions as well as any photos. By keeping notes on your Napa getaway, you can enlighten the rest of us!

_____
_____
_____
_____
_____
_____
_____
_____
_____
_____
_____
_____
_____
_____
_____
_____
_____
_____
_____
_____
_____
_____
_____
_____
_____
_____
_____
_____
_____

Share your experiences online at wineopolis.com

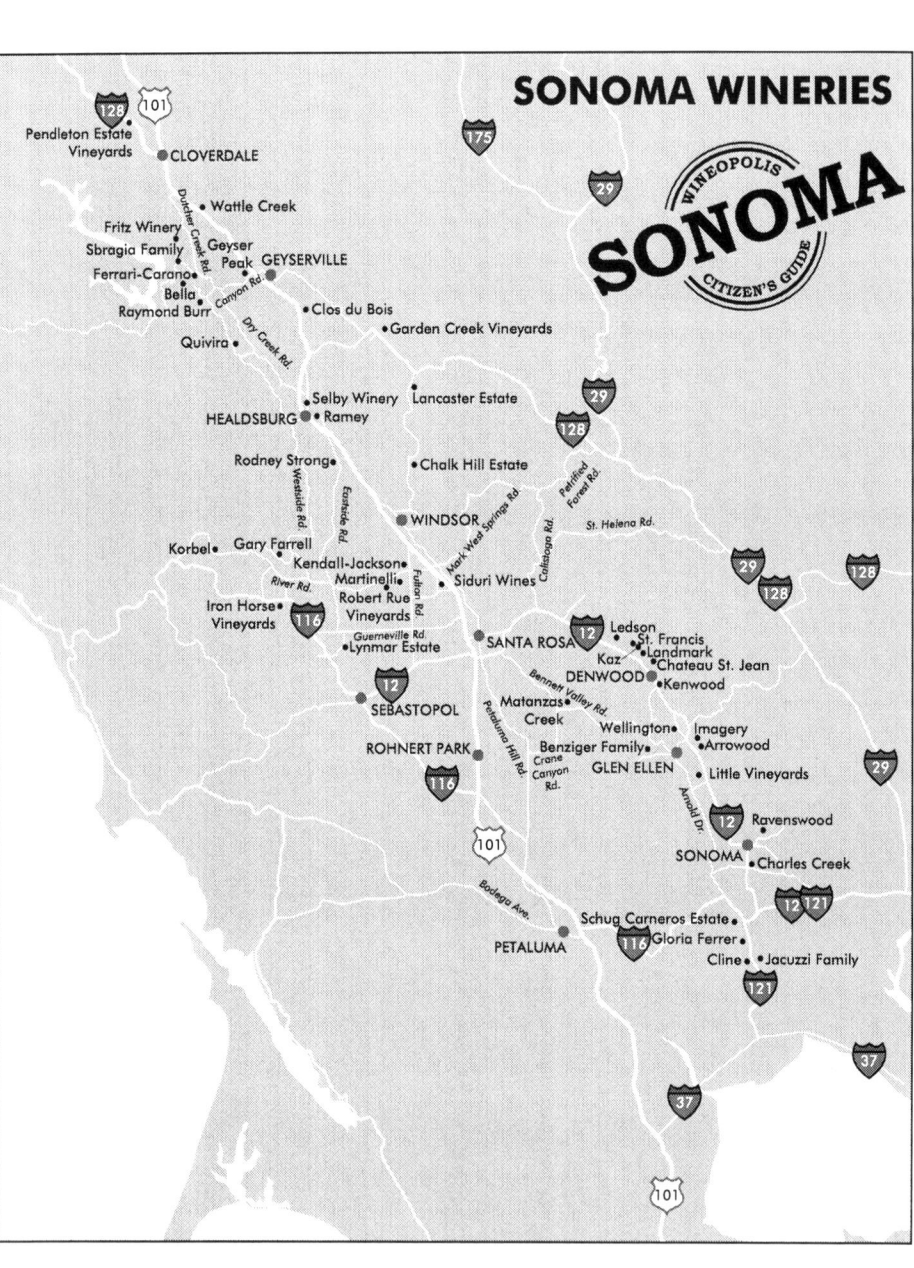

IV. EXPERIENCING SONOMA

Now that we have fully explored Napa, we turn our sights to its neighbor to the west, Sonoma County. We'll go about it in the same manner: a brief highlight of towns and appellations, a listing of our top recommended wineries, a listing of our top recommended restaurants, the top things to see and do, and finally recommendations on where to stay.

> Remember, what's great about Wineopolis is that we learn based upon the experiences of the community at large! And while we have tried to list the best places in this guide book, if you don't see your favorites listed here or if you want to share a new discovery with your fellow travelers and wine lovers, go to www.wineopolis.com where your voice can be heard. So, without further ado, let's get started.

All About Sonoma

Like its wine cousin Napa County, Sonoma County is also long and thin. It stretches from the Mayacamas mountains in the east until it ends at the coast of the Pacific Ocean in the west. Most of the population of Sonoma County (roughly 466,000 residents) lives along U.S. Highway 101 as it stretches north from San Francisco, up through Santa Rosa and on to Geyserville. Outside of the highway is mostly farmland, including fruit orchards, dairy farms, livestock and vineyards. This valley is abundant with country roads that stretch far and wide from the ocean through the rolling hills, the valley and on up into the mountains. Therefore, it's highly accessible for exploration and tasting of all the fantastic wines produced in the region. We'll start at the southern end of the valley and work our way north, describing the towns and appellations that are found along the way. First, let's look at the main cities and towns that are found within the county's borders.

Sonoma

Sonoma, though not the largest town in the county, has some of the oldest wineries in the region. It lies off of Highway 12 to the east and there are only approximately 9,800 residents, so it's not exactly a bustling city. But the town is steeped in history and the many historic sites and reason enough to visit, such as the Mission San Francisco de Solano, the Sonoma Barracks and historic Swiss Hotel (which we'll profile later). The historic central plaza (which houses the above) is about eight acres total and is home to many upscale shops and restaurants. There are also many notable wineries in close proximity, making Sonoma a popular starting off point when visiting the region.

Petaluma

Petaluma is the first city along Highway 101 as you enter the county. It's the third largest town in Sonoma with about 54,000 residents. The town is littered with charming Victorian-era houses set against some modern art deco buildings. There are a handful of wineries nearby, making this town a worthy stop.

Santa Rosa

Santa Rosa is the county seat. It sits almost dead center in the valley along Highway 101 and is also the most populated city in Sonoma County. Latest estimates have the population at around 154,000. Most notable about Santa Rosa is the effort made in environmental responsibility with many large employers in the city being eco-conscious. The bustling downtown area of Santa Rosa is conveniently split by Highway 101. There are many antique shops and historic buildings across from more modern shops, restaurants, coffee shops and souvenir shops. And yes, there are plenty of wineries nearby. If you want more of a city feel when you travel, then we suggest you stay here.

Healdsburg

As you head north on Highway 101 you next hit Healdsburg. Though Santa Rosa is the most populated town, the city of Healdsburg is currently the most popular. This community of roughly 11,000 people has become quite a hot destination in Sonoma. The charming town square is surrounded by art galleries, wine tasting rooms and many upscale specialty shops. There's even a central town gazebo where you can enjoy an outdoor concert in the summertime. But the real reason for its popularity is that it sits near three main grape-growing regions: Russian River Valley, Dry Creek Valley and Alexander Valley.

Geyserville

Geyserville lies just north of Healdsburg. It is technically an unincorporated community, taking its name from the many natural occurring steam vents found nearby. These vents (also called fumaroles) are easily spotted along the landscape, particularly during the cooler months. The area where they are found is called The Geysers and is a popular tourist attraction. Geyserville is not only perfectly situated for visiting nearby wineries but there are many outdoor activities to be enjoyed due to its proximity to Lake Sonoma.

Cloverdale

At the northern tip of the valley off of Highway 101 is the town of Cloverdale. This town has nearly 8,000 residents and boasts a rejuvenated downtown area with an expanse of shops and restaurants all within walking distance. This city is on the edge of the Alexander Valley and is near a whole host of excellent wineries. As you head north out of Cloverdale, you are met with ever expanding forests of Redwoods as you near Mendocino County. For those looking to experience the natural beauty of the California Redwoods, as well as explore some vineyards, Cloverdale offers the best of both worlds.

Other Notables

Sonoma County, being more populated than Napa, naturally has more to offer in the way of townships and planned communities. There are far more than we have room to mention, though we'll give some a shout out here. **Rohnert Park** is along Highway 101 just north of Petaluma. It started out as a small planned community and has now grown with all kinds of chain restaurants, stores and hotels. On the Pacific Ocean to the West lies **Bodega Bay**, which is one of the largest fishing ports north of San Francisco. This is where scenic Highway 1 once again meets the coast as it winds its way north towards Oregon. A very scenic area, having been the location of many movies including Alfred Hitchcock's *The Birds*, this coastal town is definitely worth a visit if you have the time.

Share your experiences online at wineopolis.com

Sebastopol is along Highway 12 as you head back inland from the coast. Named after a Russian city, this small community is famous for growing Gravenstein apples. Back up Highway 101, just north of Santa Rosa, is *Windsor*. This small community has completely revitalized its downtown area in the last few years with a theme that evokes the Old West, giving it a great picture-worthy appearance.

In the Eastern part of the valley along Highway 12 are two unincorporated communities worth mentioning. They are *Glen Ellen* and *Kenwood*. These communities are in the heart of some of the best wineries in Sonoma County and are charming places to stay if you want to experience small town life.

Now that we've laid out the land a little bit, let's talk about the appellations found in Sonoma County.

Sonoma Appellations

Sonoma is home to some of the most recognizable appellations that are held in high esteem throughout the wine community. Sonoma County has about 60,000 acres of its total one million acres that are dedicated to growing grapes. It is one of the largest wine producers in the state, far out-producing its neighboring Napa Valley. There are 14 appellations found in Sonoma County and they are all fairly prominent. However, the North Coast AVA, which covers many counties, also covers Sonoma. The most planted grape is the Chardonnay, followed by the Cabernet Sauvignon. Below is a list of the appellations found in Sonoma (in alphabetical order) so you can determine which ones you want to visit and/or look for in your local store.

Alexander Valley AVA - Alexander Valley is in the northeastern part of the valley. A portion rests on the valley floor, making it warmer than other appellations at higher elevations. This makes the soil perfect for growing Chardonnay and Cabernet Sauvignon. The eastern end of the valley is hillier and grows mostly Zinfandel and Merlot grapes.

Bennett Valley AVA – Bennett Valley lies in the southeast and produces a bulk of their grapes for well-known winery Kendall-Jackson. The climate here is somewhat cooler than other regions, making it a prime location for Merlot.

Chalk Hill AVA – In the central part of the county towards the east is Chalk Hill, which is really a sub-appellation of the Russian River Valley AVA in the foothills near the town of Windsor. The soil here is particularly volcanic and ashy, making it ideal for white wines such as Chardonnay and Sauvignon Blanc.

Dry Creek Valley AVA – Dry Creek Valley is an appellation along the Sonoma County valley floor to the north. The hallmark grape here is the Zinfandel, though the region also grows some Sauvignon Blanc, Cabernet Sauvignon as well as Bordeaux varietals.

Green Valley of Russian River Valley AVA – This is the smallest appellation in Sonoma County, also being a part of the greater Russian River Valley to the southwest. This area is known for its prominent fog, making the conditions perfect for Pinot Noir.

Knight's Valley AVA – This appellation is in the far eastern border of the county towards the Mayacamas Range and more significantly Mt. St. Helena. These high elevation vineyards are ideal for very rich Cabernet Sauvignon.

Los Carneros (also known as Carneros) AVA – The Los Carneros region has a variety of dense and shallow soils, which are good for many different varietals. This appellation spans the southern low end of the Mayacamas Mountains thus splitting the AVA between Sonoma and Napa. The Sonoma portion is known for Pinot Noir and Chardonnay, among many other varietals.

North Coast AVA – This is a very broad California appellation that covers 6 counties, including Sonoma. Since this appellation also covers many smaller appellations with much more recognizable names, most wines will carry the name of the sub-appellation unless a majority of the grapes don't come from a distinct area.

Northern Sonoma AVA – Northern Sonoma lies to the northwest of the Russian River Valley, but in reality it encompasses most of Sonoma County except those in the southeast (Sonoma Valley, Los Carneros). With such a broad range, there are many varietals that grow here.

Rockpile AVA – At the very northern tip of the county, you will find the Rockpile appellation, which is also in the northwestern tip of the Dry Creek Valley. This area gets an abundance of sunshine, therefore grapes grown here make very fruity Zinfandel.

Russian River Valley AVA – The Russian River Valley is probably the most recognized appellation in Sonoma. Because the region gets fog from the nearby Pacific coast, grapes here develop a very full flavor; the favorite being Pinot Noir and Chardonnay. The last count showed 79 wineries in this region alone.

Sonoma Coast AVA – The Sonoma Coast appellation is quite vast, encompassing pretty much all of the land along the Pacific Ocean, thereby giving this region a much cooler climate and higher rainfall, than the valley. Top grapes here are Pinot Noir, Chardonnay and Syrah.

Sonoma Mountain AVA – The small Sonoma Mountain range is what gives this appellation its name, as well as many high elevation vineyards. It is actually a part of the Sonoma Valley AVA, but the mountainous

Share your experiences online at wineopolis.com

terroir allows for a sub-appellation. Very hearty Cabernet Sauvignon grow well here, as well as Chardonnay and Zinfandel.

Sonoma Valley AVA – Sonoma Valley spans most of the southeastern part of the county. This area is also called The Valley of the Moon and is situated between two small mountain ranges. The terroir here is very unique, with the mountains keeping much of the cool Pacific air at bay. The valley region produces very fruity Chardonnay and Cabernet Sauvignon, while the hillier regions grow a hearty yet fruity Zinfandel.

Sonoma County produces a lot of wine. Though there are many different varietals found here, Sonoma is particularly well-known for Chardonnay, Cabernet Sauvignon and Zinfandel. Sonoma County, just like Napa next door, has some very exclusive, award-winning wines, which is why it is also a top destination for wine lovers.

Now let's get to the wineries!

Recommended Reading: American Vintage – The Rise of American Wine by Paul Lukacs

American Vintage…is a great read about the history of winemaking in America. It all started when Thomas Jefferson proclaimed, "We in America can make wine doubtless as good as the great wines of Europe." From our bright beginnings, to the dark times of Prohibition and through the wine renaissance of the late 20th century, this book will give you a great insight to the brief but exciting history of the vine in the U.S.A.

Share your experiences online at wineopolis.com

Sonoma Wineries: A Guide

Next we are going to highlight the best wineries Sonoma has to offer. Some are well-known behemoths of the wine world; others are smaller, more exclusive wineries off the beaten path. But again, as we only have so many pages to talk about wine, we're picking our favorites as well as the ones you definitely cannot miss. We'll go through the list geographically, starting in the southern end of the valley and zigzagging north. As always, come let us know about your trip so the community can be enriched and excited by your discoveries! Visit Wineopolis.com and tell about your Sonoma adventure!

**A reminder on how our listings are organized. We will first list the winery, its address and contact information, appellation(s), followed by a brief description of the winery, tasting room days, hours and fees, the best wines they produce, and any interesting features or facts.

Cline Cellars

24737 Highway 121 (Arnold Dr.), Sonoma, CA 94576 / 800-546-2070
www.clinecellars.com
Appellation: Los Carneros
Hours: 10am – 6pm daily (Tours daily 11am, 1pm, 3pm)
Tastings: Complimentary!

Cline Cellars has a stellar Zinfandel, especially the Ancient Vines label and it's worth the drive here to taste it. Founder Fred Cline started the winery with his inheritance money from the sale of Jacuzzi Bros. (his grandfather founded that famous company). Though originally housed in Oakley, the winery was moved in 1991 to the southern tip of Sonoma County, east of Petaluma. This winery has a quaint, country charm, with rows of rosebushes lining the path towards the main building. The grounds are dotted with several picnic benches amongst the trees, so make sure you come with a full basket. Best of all, tastings are complimentary – music to our ears.

Jacuzzi Family Winery

24724 Highway 121 (Arnold Dr.), Sonoma, CA 94576 / 866-522-8693
www.jacuzziwines.com
Appellation: Los Carneros
Hours: 10am – 5:30 pm daily
Tastings: Complimentary!

This winery is currently owned by Fred and Nancy Cline, who also own nearby Cline Cellars. Both wineries come from the famous Jacuzzi family. This winery

make notes in your Wine Log at the end of this section

pays homage to the Jacuzzi roots in the Friuli region of Italy, with the massive stone building mirroring their once ancestral home. Around the property, you can find many of the old Jacuzzi products, from airplane propellers, water well pumps, and the bath and spa products that brought the family fame. Tours are available for a fee ($15-$25 per person). This winery is known for its many Italian varietals, so try the Nebbiolo and Sangiovese, as well as the Pinot Noir and Chardonnay.

Gloria Ferrer Caves & Vineyards

23555 Highway 121 (Arnold Dr.), Sonoma, CA 94576 / 707-996-7256
www.gloriaferrer.com
Appellation: Los Carneros
Hours: 10am – 5pm daily
Tastings: $4-$10 per glass for sparkling wines, $1-$3 per glass for still wines

Gloria Ferrer is well known for their sparkling wines, especially the Brut Rosé. The Ferrer family has been making sparkling wines for over 100 years in Spain and when they wanted to expand into America, they realized the southern Sonoma region had the perfect climate for growing Chardonnay and Pinot Noir (the grapes most commonly used in sparkling wines). This winery has a strong Spanish influence in the architecture and décor, with the scenic outdoor Vista Terrace overlooking the vineyard. Stop here to try their sparkling wines, as well as their very notable still wines and tour the wine caves if you can.

Charles Creek Vineyard Tasting Room & Gallery

483 First Street West, Sonoma, CA 94576 / 707-935-3848
www.charlescreek.com
Appellation: Varied
Hours: 11am – 6pm daily
Tastings: $5 per person (applicable to wine purchase)

When hitting the shops in the town of Sonoma, don't miss out on visiting the Charles Creek Vineyard Tasting Room & Gallery. This charming antique storefront is in the middle of Sonoma's historic plaza. Once you step inside, you'll feel like you've stepped back in time to the Old West. Giving a nod to Sonoma's history, especially its Spanish roots, there are wines with names like Las Patolitas Chardonnay and La Vista Cabernet Sauvignon. This tasting room also houses an art gallery, so take a look around while you taste.

Share your experiences online at wineopolis.com

KENWOOD VINEYARDS

9592 Highway 12, Kenwood, CA 95452 / 707-833-5891
www.kenwoodvineyards.com
Appellation: Sonoma Valley
Hours: 10am – 4:30pm daily
Tastings: Complimentary or $5 for reserve wines

The most picturesque part of Kenwood Vineyards is the centuries-old barn that houses the tasting room for the winery. When the winery was first established in 1906 by the Pagani Brothers, legendary author Jack London was living and writing nearby. He was, in fact, a huge inspiration for the next batch of owners, three friends from San Francisco, who bought the property in 1970.

Today, there are grapes cultivated from the land that was once belonged to Jack London. In fact, since 1976, Kenwood Vineyards has been the exclusive producer of wines from the vineyards on the old Jack London Ranch. These wines don the wolf on the label (it was his bookplate stamp for his books) as well as London's signature. This series includes a Cabernet Sauvignon, Zinfandel, Merlot and Pinot Noir which you can taste only at the winery. The winery has another popular series called the Artist Series. On these labels, works by many contemporary artists are featured with the label changing annually. The signature wine is the Artist Series Cabernet Sauvignon and is available to taste. This series is considered a collector's wine (meaning they are rare and expensive). So that's even one more reason to come by.

Today, the winery is still housed in the ancient barn, though it has since been redesigned and houses many modern stainless steel fermenting tanks as well as upright oak barrels. Tastings here are complimentary, but for reserve wines (which you will definitely want to try) the price is a scant $5 per person. The winery features a monthly themed food and wine pairing event that is a treat, you'll want to check ahead with the winery to see when they take place.

The winery currently does not have any tours available, but if you are anxious to learn more about Jack London and his history in the region, you can visit the nearby Jack London State Historic Park. Here is a museum dedicated to the author and you can also see many old buildings and ruins from when he lived on the property.

Which wines did you taste?

Ravenswood Winery

18701 Gehricke Road, Sonoma, CA 94576 / 888-669-4679
www.ravenswood-wine.com
Appellation: Sonoma Valley
Hours: 10am – 4:30pm daily
Tastings: $10-$15 per person

Ravenswood Winery is definitely anti wine-snob. They don't believe that wine should only be for the elite. In fact, winemaker Joel Peterson believes wine is for drinking, not revering. He's our kind of guy. This winery prides itself on "No Wimpy Wines" and that's not a lie. All of their Zinfandels (14 to be exact) are hearty, thus being their specialty. They also have really good Bordeaux-style blends as well as a Petite Sirah. Come sip the wines in their laid back tasting room or outdoors on their terrace.

Schug Carneros Estate Winery

602 Bonneau Road, Sonoma, CA 94576 / 800-966-9365
www.schugwinery.com
Appellation: Los Carneros
Hours: 10am – 5pm daily
Tastings: $5 per person, $10 for reserve wines (both applicable towards purchase)

If Ravenswood is king of Zinfandel, it can be said Schug Carneros Estate Winery is king of Pinot Noir. Founder Walter Schug came from Germany

Sirah, Syrah, Say What?!?

Let's take a moment now to clear up a little confusion between Syrah and Sirah (officially called a Petite Sirah). Though they sound the same, they are not the same in essence. Let's start with Syrah. Syrah (sometimes also called Shiraz) is a dark-skinned grape which is grown to produce very rich and hearty red wines. The Syrah grape hails from the Rhône region in southeast France and is in fact a combination of two separate grape varietals: the Dureza and Mondeuse Blanche.

A Petite Sirah is made from a completely different grape called Durif (named after botanist Francois Durif) that also makes red wines, though a bit more spicy in flavor. The Petite Sirah is a popular wine in California, Israel and Australia.

So…there you have it. They are both red wines, but different grapes thus producing different notes. Now go out and buy a bottle of each and see what you like best and let your friends at Wineopolis know your results.

...tell your friends at wineopolis.com

LANDMARK VINEYARDS

101 Adobe Canyon Road, Kenwood, CA 95452 / 707-833-0218
www.landmarkwine.com
Appellation: Sonoma Valley
Hours: 10am – 4:30pm daily
Tastings: $5 per person, $10 for reserve wines, $15 for special flight

Landmark Vineyards is located at the foot of Sugarloaf Mountain, a very idyllic peak in southeastern Sonoma County in the community of Kenwood. As if taking a cue from the dramatic scenery, Landmark Vineyards has created a charming outdoor space with a 5,000 square foot courtyard (complete with fountain) where visitors can roam, mingle and take in the view all while sipping great wine.

The tasting room has an impressive vine-inspired mural behind the tasting bar, done by local artist Claudia Wagar. Here you can taste the current release wines for $5 or taste some reserve wines (available only at the winery) for $15. The winery is well-known for their Chardonnay and some other single-vineyard wines like the Pinot Noir and Syrah. There is also a vineyard tour and tasting for $15 at 11am daily, but appointments are required. The tasting room, in addition to the wine bar, has some gifts and souvenirs available for purchase.

Landmark Vineyards was founded by the great grand-daughter of legendary tractor-man John Deere, who invented the steel plow and revolutionized agriculture. The vineyard pays homage to that heritage, naming several of its vintages after family homes (the Overlook Chardonnay) and for the family legacy (the Steel Plow Syrah). The winery was built in 1989 and pays homage to its local roots by using Spanish mission-style architecture.

But, if you are here in the warm months, you really must meander around the courtyard and surrounding grounds. Past the courtyard is a great expanse of lawn that is perfect for picnics and lawn games (there's a bocce ball court, too). During the summer months, you can enjoy a tour of the vineyards by horse-drawn carriage. And if an afternoon visit is not enough, you can even stay at the winery in either their guest cottage or guest suite. Contact the winery for further details.

where did you go?

determined to make the best Pinot Noir possible. And we admit this Pinot is amazing. This estate evokes the grandeur of Europe and their tasting room has some of the best views around. Their wine is aged in a recently excavated cave system, which you can tour by appointment.

Little Vineyards Family Winery

15188 Sonoma Highway, Glen Ellen, CA 95442 / 707-996-2750
www.littlevineyards.com
Appellation: Sonoma Valley
Hours: 11am – 4:30pm Thursday-Monday
Tastings: $5 per person

This winery was begun by the Little family in 1996. They set out to produce premium red wines and they have certainly succeeded. Their Zinfandel, Syrah and Cabernet Sauvignon are all praise-worthy. But what we really love is the charming tasting room that is filled with local history. In back of the winery is a recording studio where Rich Little's band plays and records. They're a local favorite, so hopefully you'll catch them when they perform locally. Also on the grounds is a 100-year old farmhouse that was originally built by famous newspaperman William Randolph Hurst. History buffs will surely be at home here.

Benziger Family Winery

1883 London Ranch Road, Glen Ellen, CA 95442 / 888-490-2739
www.benziger.com
Appellation: Sonoma Mountain
Hours: 10am – 5pm daily
Tastings: $10 for 5 wines, $15 for 5 reserve wines, $40 for tour and tasting

High up in the mountains above Glen Ellen lies the Benziger Family Winery. What's really cool is the red tractor and attached passenger car that takes guests on a tour of the winery, vineyard and garden. There are not only grapes, but plenty of wildlife to view on this trek. The winery itself mostly produces Cabernet Sauvignon, and they are also known for many Bordeaux blends. But it is also noted that this was the first vineyard in Sonoma to become biodynamic, meaning the wine process is free of all chemicals. Don't miss out on this winery (or the tractor tour).

log it, blog it, share it at wineopolis.com

GLORIA FERRER CAVES & VINEYARDS

23555 Highway 121 (Arnold Dr.), Sonoma, CA 94576 / 707-996-7256
www.gloriaferrer.com
Appellation: Los Carneros
Hours: 10am – 5pm daily
Tastings: $4-$10 per glass for sparkling wines, $1-$3 per glass for still wines

The Ferrer family originally hails from Spain where they made sparkling wines since the late 1800s to great acclaim. When word spread about the unique terroir of the Sonoma Carneros region and its ideal conditions for Pinot Noir and Chardonnay (the main grapes used in sparkling wines), they decided to give California a try. In 1982 Gloria and José Ferrer bought the first 40 acres of land (which would later be expanded to over 200 acres). Soon after, they began planting Pinot Noir and Chardonnay.

At the time, the winery was the first champagne facility in the Carneros region. José built a Catalan-inspired house (after their home in Spain), complete with a red-tile roof and named the winery after his wife. The tasting room is indoors, but wines should really be enjoyed outside on the terrace in the warmer months. Of course, you will probably be coming to taste the sparkling wines. The best are the Brut Rosé, Carneros Cuvée, and Royal Cuvée. Even though sparkling wines are their specialty, they also have a series of still wines: Pinot Noir and Chardonnay.

Tastings here are done a little differently; they are charged by the glass. Sparkling wines are $4-$10 per glass and still wines are $1-$3 per glass. You can take a tour of the property, where you will learn about the methode champenoise which is the process of creating sparkling wines in the style of Champagnes out of France. And you can see the caves where the wine is aged. The cost of a tour is $10 per person and includes two sparkling wine tastings, so we recommend doing the tour.

But, if you want to come simply to drink by the glass, it is also worth the trip. Besides the fantastic view, there is an on-site gift shop filled with Spanish influenced trinkets. You can buy Spanish cookbooks, as well as books devoted to the region of Catalonia. There are also many locally grown products, deli items, hand-made condiments, and hand-made chocolates for purchase.

what did you see?

Imagery Estate Winery (& Art Gallery)

14335 Highway 12, Glen Ellen, CA 95442 / 877-550-4278
www.imagerywinery.com
Appellation: Sonoma Valley
Hours: 10am – 4:30pm daily
Tastings: $10 per person

Imagery Estate Winery is a sister winery to Benziger, though it couldn't be more different in look and feel. Right next to the tasting room is an art gallery, where you'll find original works from many contemporary artists. In fact, the wines themselves all have unique labels adorned with different works of art. The wines produced here hail from the local terroir and the winery uses organic and biodynamic practices. The winery prides itself on featuring varietals that may be outside the norm and may not get as much notoriety or attention as others. Some of their features include White Burgundy, Muscat, Cinsault, Mourvèdre and Malbec. These wines are also in limited production, so you really must come by to taste them and take a few home.

Arrowood Vineyards & Winery

14347 Highway 12, Glen Ellen, CA 95442 / 707-935-2600
www.arrowoodvineyards.com
Appellation: Sonoma Valley
Hours: 10am – 4:30pm daily
Tastings: $5 - $10 per person

Modeled after a New England farmhouse, the buildings of Arrowood Vineyards have some stunning wrap-around porches which offer a fantastic view of the Sonoma Valley. It feels more like a home than a winery (probably because the houses were first intended to be a bed & breakfast). Today, you can come and sip some tasty wines while taking in the scenery. There are many varietals to be had at Arrowood, so we suggest tasting as many as you can (especially their Chardonnay and Gewürztraminer).

Wellington Vineyards

11600 Dunbar Road, Glen Ellen, CA 95442 / 800-816-9463
www.wellingtonvineyards.com
Appellation: Sonoma Valley
Hours: 10am – 5pm daily (10am – 4pm in the winter)
Tastings: $5 per person

This winery is housed right in-between the hamlets of Glen Ellen and Kenwood. This is a family-run winery with a small production, but it's big on charm. Housed in a modern building with a red door, the tasting room is bright and cheerful, and filled with very friendly staff. They're known for their

post your trip photos at wineopolis.com

SCHUG CARNEROS ESTATE WINERY

602 Bonneau Road, Sonoma, CA 94576 / 800-966-9365
www.schugwinery.com
Appellation: Los Carneros
Hours: 10am – 5pm daily
Tastings: $5 per person, $10 for reserve wines (both applicable towards purchase)

Schug Carneros is known first and foremost for their Pinot Noir. The Pinot Noir grape is the hardest grape to cultivate into wine. When a winery does it well, then you simply have to taste it for yourself. When Walter Schug came to Sonoma he came here for one reason: to find the perfect climate for growing Pinot Noir. For years, he was a highly-acclaimed winemaker for Joseph Phelps, where he made Cabernet Sauvignon and eventually Pinot Noir. Loving the intensity of the Pinot Noir grape, in 1980 he decided to start his own winery and devote himself to the cultivation of a fantastic Pinot Noir and was very successful.

Now, the winery produces other good wines besides the Pinot, most notably Cabernet Sauvignon, Chardonnay, Merlot and Sauvignon Blanc. Oh, and they also produce a very good sparkling Pinot Noir that we highly recommend you taste.

The winery itself is styled after the Rhône houses of Germany, with its cris-crossed dark wood and sharp angles. In the mid-1990s they excavated an underground cave system for wine to age in giant oak barrels. The tasting room is open daily and tastings are $5 per person. For $10, you can enjoy their reserve wines. Best of all, the tasting fee is applicable to any wine purchase. Outside on their vista terrace you can take in a 360 degree view of the valley. Further down on the grounds is a European pétanque court. There are winery tours available by appointment; you'll need to check with the winery for more information.

Today, the winery is still family-run by Walter and his wife Gertrud. Son Axel works there too, handling sales. Axel's wife, Kristine, is a chef who caters special events at the winery as well as hosted dinners. Be sure to ask about her special recipes that go perfectly with the estate's wines.

Since the town of Sonoma is nearby, you're not far from the historic Sonoma Plaza and the Mission San Francisco de Solano.

sniff, taste, blog, repeat

reds, such as the Cabernet Sauvignon, Merlot and Zinfandel. But what puts this winery on our radar is their more unique wines such as the Marsanne and Roussane (which are stunning whites of the Rhône variety).

Kenwood Vineyards

9592 Highway 12, Kenwood, CA 95452 / 707-833-5891
www.kenwoodvineyards.com
Appellation: Sonoma Valley
Hours: 10am – 4:30pm daily
Tastings: Complimentary or $5 for reserve wines

The inspiration for Kenwood Vineyards' label (the wolf) comes from author Jack London, who once owned the estate next door. In fact, it was London who called this idyllic valley The Valley of the Moon. The winery itself has a rustic charm, with a centuries old barn where you can taste the best wines Kenwood has to offer (such as the Sauvignon Blanc and Zinfandel). The winery has an Artist Series Cabernet Sauvignon which is a popular collector's item if you are able to purchase it.

Landmark Vineyards

101 Adobe Canyon Road, Kenwood, CA 95452 / 707-833-0218
www.landmarkwine.com
Appellation: Sonoma Valley
Hours: 10am – 4:30pm daily
Tastings: $5 per person, $10 for reserve wines, $15 for special flight

At the center of Landmark Vineyards lies a 5,000 square foot courtyard (complete with fountain) where visitors can roam, mingle and take in the view all while sipping wine. In the distance lies Sugarloaf Mountain which looms over the winery and the nearby community of Kenwood. The inside of the tasting room is painted with an impressive vine-inspired mural by local artist Claudia Wagar. There's also a great picnic area so bring a bite and be sure to try their Chardonnay.

Chateau St. Jean

8555 Highway 12, Kenwood CA 95452 / 707-833-4134
www.chateaustjean.com
Appellation: Varied
Hours: 10am – 5pm (except major holidays)
Tastings: $10-$15 per person

If you didn't know any better, you'd swear you have just traveled to Europe when you come upon this sprawling countryside manor. This is the beauty and the grandeur of Chateau St. Jean. The best award-winning wine here is a Cabernet Sauvignon-Cabernet Franc-Malbec blend called the Cinq Cépages.

Share your experiences online at wineopolis.com

LEDSON WINERY & VINEYARD

7335 Highway 12, Santa Rosa, CA / 707-537-3810
www.ledson.com
Appellation: Sonoma Valley
Hours: 10am – 5pm daily
Tastings: $5-$15 per person, $25 for private tasting with gourmet cheeses

If you're looking to visit a European-style castle while in Wine County, you won't be disappointed when you come to Ledson Winery. This place is the definition of grand estate. In fact, the building is known locally as "the castle." The building took almost ten years to build, but the Ledson family, led by Steve, knew they were creating something special. Now initially, this grand castle was to be the Ledson family residence as they tended their Merlot vineyards (which were being sold to other wineries). But the appeal was so great, they decided to turn the building into a visiting center and tasting room. Subsequently, they started producing their own vintages and in 1997 they released their first Estate Merlot. In 1999, the winery was finally open to the public.

We will state the obvious by saying this winery is popular. The grounds outside the castle are quite extensive and host many private functions as well as weddings. Tastings range in price from $5-$15 dollars depending on the vintages. There is a private tasting, along with gourmet cheese, for $25. The specialty here is the Merlot, as well as the Cabernet Sauvignon, Chardonnay and Zinfandel.

But don't miss out on seeing the building itself. There are only 12 rooms available to be seen by the public, but they are quite grand. This includes nine tasting rooms (yes nine), a parlor, club room, and gourmet marketplace where you can buy meats, cheeses and even sandwiches, salads and desserts. So plan on having lunch when you come here. You can eat inside in the parlor (complete with marble fireplace) or outside on picnic tables overlooking the grounds.

The Ledsons also own a hotel right on Sonoma's historic plaza called the Ledson Hotel and Harmony Lounge. We strongly recommend staying here if you will be visiting the town of Sonoma. This family knows luxury and the hotel is every bit as grand as the winery estate.

what did you like?

It's a wine worth traveling to taste. Outside is their new Visitors Center in a sprawling Mediterranean garden which is perfect for an afternoon picnic. They also have a very notable Chardonnay and Cabernet Sauvignon.

Kaz Winery

233 Adobe Canyon Road, Kenwood, CA 95452 / 877-833-2536
www.kazwinery.com
Appellation: Sonoma Valley
Hours: 11am – 5pm Friday-Monday
Tastings: $5 per person

Kaz Winery is a fun, down-home and laid-back experience that you cannot miss. This small family-run winery prides itself on great wine and a great sense of humor. Rick Kasmier had been making wine in his basement when he finally decided to give winemaking an official try, opening Kaz Winery in the mid-1990s. When you come here you're treated like family with no air of formality whatsoever. They have a variety of good reds, mostly rare varietals, as well as ports. Come for a good laugh and a good wine.

Siduri Wines

980 Airway Ct., Suite C, Santa Rosa, CA 95403 / 707-578-3882
www.novyfamilywines.com
Appellation: Varied
Hours: 10am – 3pm daily by appointment
Tastings: Complimentary!

Siduri Wines does not look like your typical winery with grand signs, expansive lawns and mansion-like buildings. This winery is serious about wines and it shows. The winery is in a warehouse in a section of town surrounded by restaurants and chain stores. Appointments are required, which means you won't have to rub elbows with a large crowd and instead can get serious about tasting the wines. Their best is a single-vineyard Pinot Noir and Syrah, though the Pinot is their pride and joy.

St. Francis Winery & Vineyards

100 Pythian Road, Santa Rosa, CA 95409 / 888-675-9463
www.stfranciswinery.com
Appellation: Sonoma Valley
Hours: 10am – 5pm daily
Tastings: $10 per person, $30 for food and wine pairing

This winery was one of the first in Wine Country to offer an extensive food and wine pairing and they are still going strong. St. Francis has a gourmet chef on staff to continually innovate new and exciting dishes to complement

let us know your favorites at wineopolis.com

CHATEAU ST. JEAN

8555 Highway 12, Kenwood CA 95452 / 707-833-4134
www.chateaustjean.com
Appellation: Varied
Hours: 10am – 5pm (except major holidays)
Tastings: $10-$15 per person

Another winery that is reminiscent of a grand European estate is Chateau St. Jean, located in southern Sonoma Valley. The Chateau was originally built in the1920s as a summer home for the Goff family, originally from Michigan. Because of prohibition, grape growing was abandoned and the family grew prunes and walnuts on the land. It wasn't until the 1970s that the building was purchased by a California family and converted to a winery. Since the building has been immaculately preserved and dedicated in memory to the Goff family (there are two ponds shaped as Lake Huron and Lake Michigan), it has since been listed by the National Trust for Historic Preservation.

The Chateau itself is a sight to see, as well as the expansive landscaped gardens done in a Mediterranean style. You can spend an entire afternoon strolling the lush grounds and fountains. In the central fountain, you'll find a sculpture of "St. Jean" that is fashioned after a family member (and thus the winery name). Visitors are welcome to picnic here on good weather days (we suggest buying a bottle to go with your lunch). There are some picnic tables available, but the grass is just as comfortable.

The winery believes in having vineyard-exclusive wines, so their wines all carry the name of a specific appellation. The most notable is the Cinq Cépages, which is a Cabernet Sauvignon-Cabernet Franc-Malbec blend. There's also a Cinq Cépages Cabernet Sauvignon. Tastings are $10 per person and are held in the main tasting room inside the expansive Visitors Center. For $15, you can taste their reserve wines inside the Chateau in the Reserve Tasting Room.

The Chateau has daily tours of the gardens and the Chateau which also includes a tasting. A reservation for the tour is strongly recommended.

find free resources at wineopolis.com

the wines. This winery was built to resemble an early California mission and its name is a reference to St. Francis of Assisi. You can taste wines inside or out on the patio overlooking nearby Hood Mountain. Be sure to try the Chardonnay and Cabernet Sauvignon.

Ledson Winery & Vineyard

7335 Sonoma Hwy (Hwy 12), Kenwood, CA 95409 / 707-537-3810
www.ledson.com
Appellation: Sonoma Valley
Hours: 10am – 5pm daily
Tastings: $5-$15 per person, $25 for private tasting with gourmet cheeses

We don't know what's more impressive, the Cabernet Sauvignon or the Cathedral-style castle looming majestically above rows of grape vines. What's even more impressive than the building are the expansive grounds just outside, which are perfect for picnics. Inside there are a few tasting rooms as well as a gift boutique and gourmet market. Ledson is best known for their Chardonnay and Merlot, but our favorite is the Johannisberg Riesling.

Matanzas Creek Winery

6097 Bennett Valley Road, Santa Rosa, CA 95404 / 800-590-6464
www.matanzascreek.com
Appellation: Bennett Valley, Sonoma Valley
Hours: 10am – 4:30pm daily
Tastings: $5 per person

Named for the nearby stream, Matanzas Creek Winery sits in the middle of Bennett Valley. The winery had an overhaul in 1985 after the increase in popularity of its smoky Merlot as well as its Chardonnay. Many years later, the winery is continuing to grow. Originally built on an old dairy farm, just outside the main building is an acre planted entirely with lavender, making for a beautiful and great smelling location. (Stop by the gift shop for lavender products galore).

Lynmar Estate

3909 Frei Road, Sebastopol, CA 95472 / 707-829-3374
www.lynmarestate.com
Appellation: Russian River Valley
Hours: 10am – 5pm daily
Tastings: $10 per person ($25 for reserve wines)

Lynmar Estate is the perfect place to come spend a few hours sipping wines under an umbrella on their outdoor terrace or roam the nearby watershed

make notes in your Wine Log at the end of this section

ST. FRANCIS WINERY & VINEYARDS

100 Pythian Road, Santa Rosa, CA 95409 / 888-675-9463
www.stfranciswinery.com
Appellation: Sonoma Valley
Hours: 10am – 5pm daily
Tastings: $10 per person, $30 for food and wine pairing

The St. Francis Winery is not only known for good wines, they were an early innovator in offering food and wine pairings to the public. The tradition still goes strong today, as the winery has an executive chef on staff to continually create innovative cuisines that pair perfectly with the estate wines. People come here from all over to taste and sip, while taking in the beauty of Sonoma Valley. The name comes from St. Francis de Assisi, as tribute to his role as a protector of the land. There is a statue of him on the grounds.

The main Visitors Center is crafted after the early Spanish missions that once dotted the landscape, with its sand-colored stucco walls, red tile roof, and looming bell tower. Outside is the Wild Oak Vineyard framed by Hood Mountain in the distance. Walking the grounds, you'll get a whiff of lavender from the many lavender bushes that line the walkways.

Tastings are held either inside the Visitors Center or outside on the terrace. For $10 per person, you can taste four current release wines. For $15, you can taste some small production wines that are only available at the winery. Or for $15, you can experience a Zin Tasting, which offers you a taste of different Zinfandels (a specialty). Besides the Zin, St. Francis is also known for their Cabernet Sauvignon, Chardonnay, Merlot as well as a Port and Rosé.

However, you really need to come experience the food. For $30, you can enjoy a food and wine pairing. It consists of four gourmet appetizers paired with wines served tableside. Some past menus include a range of foods from mini cheeseburgers to baked brie crepes. The menu changes seasonally, but they always use the best local ingredients available. From June through October, you can enjoy a Wine & Charcuterie, which includes many pâtés, cheeses and other meats.

If you are around on the weekend, you can take their 'Wine-Cations' tour (like a vacation), a winery tour as well as a Library Tasting of exclusive wines held in their wine cave.

Share your experiences online at wineopolis.com

filled with all sorts of mammals, birds, reptiles and plants. Well, there's also the leather couches inside the tasting room, but no matter where you drink, you're in for a relaxing treat. The primary grape varieties grown here are Chardonnay and Pinot Noir. You can also opt to take a tour along with a wine tasting paired with food ($45-$65 per person). This is not a very touristy winery (no gift shop) so you can expect some one-on-one attention from the winery's staff.

Iron Horse Vineyards

9786 Ross Station Road, Sebastopol, CA 9572 / 707-887-1507
www.ironhorsevineyards.com
Appellation: Green Valley
Hours: 10am – 3:30pm daily
Tastings: $10 per person

The drive leading up to Iron Horse Vineyards is as much a part of the experience as the wine itself. First, you'll cross a small bridge, then make your way up an oak-lined drive which opens up to olive and palm trees before hitting a rustic building which houses the winery. The tasting room is outdoors, so you can best take in the stunning scenery. There are no bells and whistles here. It is a working vineyard and the owners live on site. What you will find is some down-home hospitality by which to enjoy some great sparkling wines as well as their still wines including Pinot Noir and Chardonnay.

Kendall-Jackson Wine Center

5007 Fulton Road, Fulton, California 95439 / 866-287-9818
www.kj.com
Appellation: Varied
Hours: 10am – 5pm daily (garden tours 11am, 1pm, 3pm daily)
Tastings: $5-$15 per person

Kendall-Jackson is synonymous with good wine. They have a massive production and chances are you've had more than a few of their wines as they produce just about all of the most popular wine varietals. In Sonoma, just outside of Santa Rosa, you can visit their Wine Center for a wine and food pairing experience. The Center lies on 120 acres of gardens and vineyards, with a large European-inspired chateau in the middle. Here you can enjoy a wine tasting, wine and food pairing, tour of the grounds or all of the above.

Which wines did you taste?

CLINE CELLARS

24737 Highway 121 (Arnold Dr.), Sonoma, CA 94576 / 800-546-2070
www.clinecellars.com
Appellation: Los Carneros
Hours: 10am – 6pm daily (Tours daily 11am, 1pm, 3pm)
Tastings: Complimentary!

Cline Cellars specializes in different Zinfandel and other Rhône varietals (from Germany), such as Marsanne (full-bodied white), Rousanne (fruity white wine), Grenache (fruity red wine) and Mourvèdre (a deep red). It's a standout in the region and a good reason to come taste the wines here, though there are plenty of other reasons, we assure you. The home on the property was originally that of Fred Cline's grandmother Valeriano Jacuzzi (yes, of spa fame) back when the land was used for farming as well as fruit orchards and vineyards.

The house has been preserved, keeping its country feel and wrap-around porches. The grounds are also a treat. There are nearly fifty rosebushes lining the pathways and when they bloom, they explode with color and aroma. Cline started the winery back in 1982 at another location in Oakley, California and in 1991, the winery was relocated to its current location in Sonoma. Many of the vines grown here are some of the oldest vines in the state and makes for very rich and bold wines (the Zinfandel, Mourvèdre, and Ancient Vines Carignane).

When you come here, tastings are complimentary (yea!) and you can enjoy them in the tasting room or out on the grounds. There is a reserve tasting (for a fee). There are picnic tables too, so you'll want to come prepared with a picnic basket.

Another interesting facet to this property, however, is the on-site museum. In 1998, Nancy Cline bought a collection of perfectly scaled models of all of the California Spanish missions. It's really a treat to see them in their original glory from the time when Spain tried to convert the local Indians to Catholicism. The collection is housed in the museum located behind the tasting room.

There are also three tours available daily, so if you're here, you might want to join in.

...tell your friends at wineopolis.com

Robert Rue Vineyard

1406 Wood Road, Fulton, CA 95439 / 707-578-1601
www.robertruevineyard.com
Appellation: Russian River Valley
Hours: Appointment only
Tastings: Complimentary

To put it in owner Robert Rue's words, "we believe in nurturing our century old vines the same way we do our family – with lots of love and attention." And you'll get plenty of personalized attention here. There are no flashy signs or large looming buildings. Instead, you'll find a small, rustic farmhouse surrounded by gorgeous flower gardens. They only produce one wine; the reserve Zinfandel, but it is exquisite. So come meet the family and tour the winery, you'll have a pleasant time.

Martinelli Winery

3360 River Road, Windsor, CA 95492 / 800-346-1627
www.martinelliwinery.com
Appellation: Russian River Valley
Hours: 10am – 5pm daily
Tastings: Complimentary!

The family run Martinelli Winery is housed in a very picturesque red hop kiln barn (used for drying hops for brewing) so get your cameras ready. The winery specializes in Zinfandels, but they also have a great Chardonnay and Muscat Alexandria. The vineyard itself was formerly called Jackass Hill vineyard (an old family joke). Today, you can sip the wines in the rustic barn or out on the weathered wooden benches under a vine-covered trellis.

Lancaster Estate Winery

15001 Chalk Hill Road, Healdsburg, CA 95448 / 707-433-8178
www.lancaster-estate.com
Appellation: Alexander Valley
Hours: 10am – 4pm Monday-Saturday
Tastings: Complimentary (appointment only)

Lancaster Estate Winery is another small family-owned winery perched in the scenic Alexander Valley. Their specialty is in growing the Cabernet grape. To say their Cabernet Sauvignon is exceptional is an understatement, though recently they have also produced a tasty Sauvignon Blanc. Tours include the winery, underground caves and a tasting. You will need to plan ahead since the winery tours are by appointment only and is quite popular among many wine lovers.

where did you go?

JACUZZI FAMILY WINERY

24724 Highway 121 (Arnold Dr.), Sonoma, CA 94576 / 866-522-8693
www.jacuzziwines.com
Appellation: Los Carneros
Hours: 10am – 5:30 pm daily
Tastings: Complimentary!

The Jacuzzi Family Winery is owned by Fred and Nancy Cline, who also own nearby Cline Cellars. They are part of the famous Jacuzzi family, who made their fortune first in airplane propellers before moving to water pumps and the bath and spa products that bear the family name. This winery pays homage to the family and is designed after their ancestral home in Friuli, Italy. (Though from a distance, it looks like a majestic, stone castle). There is an Italian influence everywhere you look, such as the ornate Venetian-style glass chandeliers and prominent Italian art. The buildings surround an interior courtyard with a marble fountain (complete with a statue of Neptune on his water horses that spout water) as well as marble statues framing the archways.

When you first enter the building, you'll marvel at the grand entranceway with beamed ceiling. To the left is the tasting room, elegantly appointed with tables and benches for seating, as well as some products and souvenirs available for purchase in the adjacent gift shop. The tastings here, like at nearby Cline Cellars, are complimentary. The winery is known for many Italian varietals (not a surprise), especially the red wines, with standouts being a Barbera and Nebbiolo (rich red wines), Muscato (a fruity white), Valeriano (a red named after a family matriarch) and Sangiovese (a spicy red). They also have a good Merlot, Cabernet Sauvignon, and Chardonnay.

This property is also home to The Olive Press; a producer of some first rate olive oil from local olive groves. The shop has a tasting bar where you can taste different oils, as well as a gift shop including olive oil and other olive-themed condiments. You can even visit the olive pressing facility and witness olive oil being made. There are tours available, but you will need to call ahead to inquire.

On the second floor of the building, you'll find a small family history museum, where you can see early Jacuzzi products as well as other family memorabilia.

log it, blog it, share it at wineopolis.com

Chalk Hill Estate Winery

10300 Chalk Hill Road, Healdsburg, CA 95448 / 800-838-4306
www.chalkhill.com
Appellation: Chalk Hill, Russian River Valley
Hours: 10am – 4pm daily (by appointment)
Tastings: $10 per person

Chalk Hill estate winery has all the makings of a European grand estate. Though small and exclusive, you'll get an experience here like no other. If you sign up for a Culinary Tour you are in for a treat complete with a tour of the vineyards and garden, as well as a tasting paired with gourmet food in their regal grand pavilion. You will have to pay for this pampering ($75) but your taste buds will thank you. The winery sprawls over several thousand acres and is almost like a community unto itself as much as a winery. You'll want to try their Estate Cabernet Sauvignon and Chardonnay.

Ramey Wine Cellars

25 Healdsburg Avenue, Healdsburg, CA 95448 / 707-433-0870
www.rameywine.com
Appellation: Russian River Valley
Hours: 10am – 2pm Monday-Friday by appointment
Tastings: $25 per person (for 6-8 wines)

David Ramey was a winemaker for many notable wineries such as Matanzas Creek and Chalk Hill. And in 1996, he and his wife decided to branch out and start their own operation. Today, Ramey Wine Cellars is located in the heart of Healdsburg and their grapes are sourced from the many vineyards David has worked at over the years. When you come to their tasting room, you can enjoy a wide variety of reds and whites, including their specialty Chardonnay and Cabernet Sauvignon.

Selby Winery

215 Center Street, Healdsburg, CA 95448 / 707-431-1288
www.selbywinery.com
Appellation: Russian River Valley
Hours: 11am – 5pm daily
Tastings: $5 per person

The Selby Winery tasting room is located in a small vine-covered cottage on a side street off of the main plaza in the town of Healdsburg. Owner Susie Selby left corporate America to follow her dreams of being a winemaker and has since led the way with creating some award-winning wines. So when in town, take a break from shopping at the plaza nearby and come try her Sauvignon Blanc, Merlot, Syrah or Rosé (from Pinot Noir grapes).

what did you see?

Rodney Strong Vineyards

11455 Old Redwood Highway, Healdsburg, CA 95448 / 800-678-4763
www.rodneystrong.com
Appellation: Varied
Hours: 10am – 5pm daily (also open for self guided tours)
Tastings: Complimentary (small fee for reserve wines)

If you're looking for dramatic architecture and landscape, then come to Rodney Strong Vineyards. This dynamic winery has a one of a kind building (it looks like an eagle about to take flight) and a beautiful garden complete with a pond and mini waterfall. If you're looking to picnic, this is a perfect spot. They have some excellent vintages here such as their Sauvignon Blanc and Cabernet Sauvignon. In the summer, Rodney Strong Winery holds a summer concert series with some notable musical performers. This winery is also a popular spot for outdoor weddings.

Ferrari-Carano Vineyards & Winery

8761 Dry Creek Road, Healdsburg, CA 95448 / 707-433-6700
www.ferrari-carano.com
Appellation: Dry Creek Valley
Hours: 10am – 5pm daily
Tastings: $5 for classic wines, $15 for reserve wines, $20-$30 for private tastings

Owners Don and Rhonda Carano were hotel owners from Reno, Nevada who came to Sonoma to learn the art of fine winemaking. Well, they certainly have succeeded. They are now known for a Siena Sangiovese blend as well as a Fumé Blanc, Pinot Grigio, and PreVail Cabernet Sauvignon. The grand estate is one not to be missed. It's an Italian-inspired mansion overlooking several well-landscaped gardens. When you're here at the right time, you can witness more than 10,000 tulips and daffodils in bloom.

Quivira Vineyards & Winery

4900 West Dry Creek Road, Healdsburg, CA 95448 / 707-431-8333
www.quivirawine.com
Appellation: Dry Creek Valley
Hours: 11am – 5pm daily
Tastings: $5 per person (applicable to wine purchase)

This winery was designated fully organic in 2005 and is revered for its biodynamic practices. Quivira (key-veer-ah) Vineyards is a small production winery, using the special qualities of the soil to grow grapes perfectly suited to the climate. These in turn make some excellent wines, such as a Sauvignon Blanc, Zinfandel and Petite Sirah. You will not be disappointed with the scenery here. As you sip wines out on their patio, you can take in the grandeur of their rolling vineyards leading up to Mt. St. Helena. A true feast for the senses.

post your trip photos at wineopolis.com

Gary Farrell Winery

10701 Westside Road, Healdsburg, CA 95448 / 707-473-2900
www.garyfarrellwines.com
Appellation: Russian River Valley
Hours: 11am – 4pm daily
Tastings: $5 - $15 per person

Gary Farrell Winery lies near the top of scenic Westside Road as you near Healdsburg. You cannot miss the entrance with its giant stone pillars holding up a wooden trellis. This winery mirrors the natural beauty of the surrounding landscape, giving the place a woodsy sort of ambiance. The tasting room window shows dramatic views of sloping hillsides filled with oak and redwood trees. Enjoy the view while sipping their Chardonnay and Pinot Noir.

Raymond Burr Vineyards

8339 W. Dry Creek Rd, Healdsburg, CA 95448 / 707-433-8559
www.raymondburrvineyards.com
Appellation: Dry Creek Valley
Hours: 11am – 5pm daily
Tastings: Complimentary

The Raymond Burr Vineyards was originally started in the late 1980s as a partnership between Burr and fellow actor Robert Benevides after having met on the set of the hit TV show *Perry Mason*. Both actors had a love of wine and decided to give winemaking a go, lucky for us. This winery is towards the end of Dry Creek Valley and besides having stunning rows of vineyards, it also has a handful of greenhouses growing all varieties of orchids (tour if you can). The orchid tour is available on weekends by appointment. The specialty wine here is the Hillside Vineyard Cabernet Sauvignon.

Bella Vineyards And Wine Caves

9711 W. Dry Creek Rd., Healdsburg, CA 95448 / 866-572-3552
www.bellawinery.com
Appellation: Dry Creek Valley
Hours: 11am – 4:30pm daily
Tastings: $5 per person

Bella Vineyards is housed in a newly refurbished red barn set among some impressive olive trees. This winery is decidedly low key, offering their tastings not in a grand tasting room, but inside their hillside wine-aging caves. Don't be fooled by the word cave. Inside you'll find an elegant setting with bistro tables lined with candelabras and ornate table settings. And, you'll get a view of the winemaking and barrel area. You'll want to taste their Zinfandel, Grenache and Syrah.

sniff, taste, blog, repeat

Clos Du Bois

19410 Geyserville Avenue, Geyserville, CA 95441 / 800-222-3189
www.closdubois.com
Appellation: Dry Creek Valley, Alexander Valley
Hours: 10am – 4:30pm daily
Tastings: $10 per person

Clos Du Bois began in Sonoma Valley and today is one of the biggest producers in the region at over three million cases annually. There are plenty of great wines to taste, including their Chardonnay, Sauvignon Blanc, and Pinot Noir. But even better, in their tasting room you can try the Jerry Garcia (of Grateful Dead fame) line of wines, complete with his colorful drawings on the label. If you come here, make sure to also take their demonstration vineyard and barrel tasting tour for $15. Around the property, the winery has some beautifully crafted gazebos that make for a perfect outdoor lunch.

Garden Creek Ranch Vineyard Winery

2335 Geysers Road, Geyserville, CA 95441 / 707-433-8345
www.gardencreekvineyards.com
Appellation: Alexander Valley
Hours: Appointment only
Tastings: Varies by request

This new small winery is gaining some attention thanks to its Bordeaux-style red called Tesserae (referring to the small pieces of tile that are used for mosaics). Owners Justin and Karin Miller are new winemakers, so it is a great opportunity to see a winery "start-up". The winery is solar-powered and the building is made from mostly recycled materials. They also use biodynamic techniques in their vineyards. Be sure to contact them ahead of time to make an appointment to come taste the wines and take a stroll around the property.

Geyser Peak Winery

22281 Chianti Road, Geyserville, CA 95441 / 800-255-9463
www.geyserpeakwinery.com
Appellation: Alexander Valley
Hours: 10am – 5pm daily
Tastings: $5 - $10 per person

Geyser Peak is one of Sonoma's oldest wineries, having first been started in 1880. They are primarily known for their whites, such as the Chardonnay and Sauvignon Blanc, but we really love their Merlot as well. The winery sits on a hillside opposite Geyser Peak mountain and has many great picnic spots along the grounds. We suggest the special reserve tasting which overlooks the barrel room (for $10 per person).

Share your experiences online at wineopolis.com

Sbragia Family Vineyards

9990 Dry Creek Road, Geyserville, CA 95441 / 707-473-2992
www.sbragia.com
Appellation: Dry Creek Valley
Hours: 11am – 5pm daily
Tastings: $5 for standard tasting, $10 for reserve tasting

Ed Sbragia, owner of Sbragia Family Vineyards, had produced several award-winning wines at Beringer over his long career (especially the 1986 Cabernet Sauvignon and the 1994 Chardonnay). Before leaving, he applied his skills to his own line of wines under the family name and the Sbragia Family Vineyards were born. This modern facility is perched upon a hill overlooking Dry Creek Valley, so sitting outside on the patio is highly recommended. Their specialties include a Chardonnay, Cabernet Sauvignon and Zinfandel.

Korbel Champagne Cellars

13250 River Road, Guerneville, CA / 800-656-7235
www.korbel.com
Appellation: Varied
Hours: 10:30am – 4:30pm daily (Deli 10am – 5pm)
Tastings: Complimentary!

If you're a champagne drinker, then you have probably heard of or tried Korbel. Started by three brothers from Czechoslovakia, Korbel has been synonymous with fantastic champagnes ever since. Korbel's red brick building has been standing since 1886. When visiting here, not only can you taste their signature bubbly, you can also tour the champagne cellars and beautifully manicured rose garden. Even though not produced in the Champagne region of France, Korbel uses the *methode champenoise* which gives it that unique flavor. BTW: there's also a deli on site, so you can enjoy a bit nearby.

Wattle Creek Winery

25510 River Road, Cloverdale, CA 95425 / 707-894-5166
www.wattlecreek.com
Appellation: Alexander Valley
Hours: Appointment only
Tastings: Call for appointment and information

Wattle Creek Winery is a family winery nestled in the northeastern part of the county by the Russian River. Wine tasting here takes place in a quiet poolside cottage, giving the whole experience a very relaxed feel. When you

what did you like?

come here, you are treated as a special guest. Since this winery is visited by appointment only, you'll avoid the crowds of larger tasting rooms and you'll really get a chance to talk with the owners about the wines as you leisurely sip and taste some of their gourmet cheeses. Try the Viognier, Pinot Noir and Cabernet Sauvignon. Definitely worth the trip if you can make it north. If not, they also have a tasting room open daily in San Francisco's Ghirardelli Square.

Fritz Winery

24691 Dutcher Creek Road, Cloverdale, CA 95425 / 800-418-9463
www.fritzwinery.com
Appellation: Dry Creek Valley
Hours: 10:30am – 4:30pm daily
Tastings: $5 per person

This family-owned and run winery is perched on the side of a hill in Dry Creek Valley, giving it some amazing subterranean space for winemaking and aging. The family dammed a local spring to create Lake Fritz, which is enjoyed from afar while sipping wines on their tasting room balcony. The winery is known for their Chardonnay, Cabernet Sauvignon and Pinot Noir. This is a great place to visit when you want to get away from the bustle of the nearby town for a peaceful, quiet afternoon.

Pendleton Estate Vineyards And Winery

35100 Highway 128, Cloverdale, CA 95425 / 707-894-3732
www.pendletonwines.com
Appellation: Alexander Valley
Hours: By appointment only
Tastings: Call for appointment and information

Pendleton Estate Vineyards is a small family winery located on some of the last pieces of land before you enter Mendocino County. You may not be planning on heading this far north in Sonoma County, but if you do, you must visit this winery. Being small, this winery offers a nice one-on-one tasting experience that can be an all afternoon affair. They have very good hand-crafted wines and since they are in very small production, you'll want to make sure to taste what you can, especially the Zinfandel and Petite Sirah. Though few, their wines are almost all award winning.

let us know your favorites at wineopolis.com

Wine Log: My Wine Notes

Winery: _____

Wine: white   red   rosé   sparkling

Name: _____

Vintage: _____

Varietal: _____

Price: _____

Body:	Simple	Moderately Complex	Complex
Acidity:	Low	Medium	High
Sweetness:	Dry	Off-dry	Sweet
Finish:	Short	Moderate	Long

Aromas & Flavors:

Whites/Roses

Citrus	Lemon, Grapefruit, Orange, Tangerine
Tree Fruit	Pear, Apple, Apricot, Peach, Nectarine
Tropical	Melon, Pineapple, Passion fruit, Banana, Mango
Floral	Geranium, Violet, Rose, Orange Blossom,
Herbal	Sage, Mint, Tea, Cut green grass
Mineral	Stone, Slate, Flint, Chalk
Spicy	Cinnamon, Nutmeg, Clove, Spiced Apple, Ginger
Nutty	Walnut, Almond, Hazelnut
Woody	Vanilla, Oak, Toast, Coconut
Yeast	Baked Bread, Bread Dough, Pie Crust
Caramel	Butter, Honey, Caramel, Butterscotch, Crème Brûlee
Other	Fuel/Diesel

Reds

Berry	Blackberry, Raspberry, Strawberry, Blueberry
Tree Fruit	Red Cherry, Black Cherry, Plum
Dried Fruit	Raisin, Fig, Prune, Berry Jam
Floral	Geranium, Violet, Rose
Herbal	Bell Pepper, Olive, Eucalyptus, Mint, Sage
Earth	Mushroom, Mineral, Forest floor
Meat	Smoked Meat, Bacon, Leather
Spice	Cinnamon, Clove, Black Pepper, Licorice/Anise
Woody	Vanilla, Oak, Cedar, Toast, Charred Wood, Tobacco
Caramel	Chocolate, Mocha, Molasses, Honey, Butterscotch
Other	Pencil Lead, Tar

Notes: _____

_____

_____

Rating

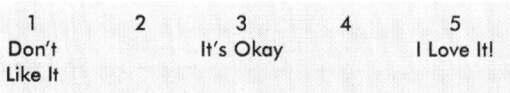

1	2	3	4	5
Don't Like It		It's Okay		I Love It!

find free resources at wineopolis.com

Wine Log: My Wine Notes

Winery: _____

Wine: white   red   rosé   sparkling

Name: _____

Vintage: _____

Varietal: _____

Price: _____

Body:	Simple	Moderately Complex	Complex
Acidity:	Low	Medium	High
Sweetness:	Dry	Off-dry	Sweet
Finish:	Short	Moderate	Long

Aromas & Flavors:

Whites/Roses

Citrus	Lemon, Grapefruit, Orange, Tangerine
Tree Fruit	Pear, Apple, Apricot, Peach, Nectarine
Tropical	Melon, Pineapple, Passion fruit, Banana, Mango
Floral	Geranium, Violet, Rose, Orange Blossom,
Herbal	Sage, Mint, Tea, Cut green grass
Mineral	Stone, Slate, Flint, Chalk
Spicy	Cinnamon, Nutmeg, Clove, Spiced Apple, Ginger
Nutty	Walnut, Almond, Hazelnut
Woody	Vanilla, Oak, Toast, Coconut
Yeast	Baked Bread, Bread Dough, Pie Crust
Caramel	Butter, Honey, Caramel, Butterscotch, Crème Brûlee
Other	Fuel/Diesel

Reds

Berry	Blackberry, Raspberry, Strawberry, Blueberry
Tree Fruit	Red Cherry, Black Cherry, Plum
Dried Fruit	Raisin, Fig, Prune, Berry Jam
Floral	Geranium, Violet, Rose
Herbal	Bell Pepper, Olive, Eucalyptus, Mint, Sage
Earth	Mushroom, Mineral, Forest floor
Meat	Smoked Meat, Bacon, Leather
Spice	Cinnamon, Clove, Black Pepper, Licorice/Anise
Woody	Vanilla, Oak, Cedar, Toast, Charred Wood, Tobacco
Caramel	Chocolate, Mocha, Molasses, Honey, Butterscotch
Other	Pencil Lead, Tar

Notes: _____

_____

_____

Rating

1	2	3	4	5
Don't Like It		It's Okay		I Love It!

Share your experiences online at wineopolis.com

Wine Log: My Wine Notes

Winery: _____

Wine: white   red   rosé   sparkling

Name: _____

Vintage: _____

Varietal: _____

Price: _____

Body:	Simple	Moderately Complex	Complex
Acidity:	Low	Medium	High
Sweetness:	Dry	Off-dry	Sweet
Finish:	Short	Moderate	Long

Aromas & Flavors:

Whites/Roses

Citrus	Lemon, Grapefruit, Orange, Tangerine
Tree Fruit	Pear, Apple, Apricot, Peach, Nectarine
Tropical	Melon, Pineapple, Passion fruit, Banana, Mango
Floral	Geranium, Violet, Rose, Orange Blossom,
Herbal	Sage, Mint, Tea, Cut green grass
Mineral	Stone, Slate, Flint, Chalk
Spicy	Cinnamon, Nutmeg, Clove, Spiced Apple, Ginger
Nutty	Walnut, Almond, Hazelnut
Woody	Vanilla, Oak, Toast, Coconut
Yeast	Baked Bread, Bread Dough, Pie Crust
Caramel	Butter, Honey, Caramel, Butterscotch, Crème Brûlee
Other	Fuel/Diesel

Reds

Berry	Blackberry, Raspberry, Strawberry, Blueberry
Tree Fruit	Red Cherry, Black Cherry, Plum
Dried Fruit	Raisin, Fig, Prune, Berry Jam
Floral	Geranium, Violet, Rose
Herbal	Bell Pepper, Olive, Eucalyptus, Mint, Sage
Earth	Mushroom, Mineral, Forest floor
Meat	Smoked Meat, Bacon, Leather
Spice	Cinnamon, Clove, Black Pepper, Licorice/Anise
Woody	Vanilla, Oak, Cedar, Toast, Charred Wood, Tobacco
Caramel	Chocolate, Mocha, Molasses, Honey, Butterscotch
Other	Pencil Lead, Tar

Notes: _____

_____

_____

Rating

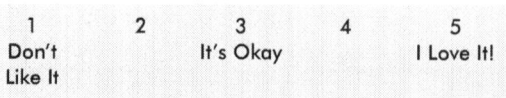

1	2	3	4	5
Don't Like It		It's Okay		I Love It!

Which wines did you taste?

Wine Log: My Wine Notes

Winery: _____
Wine: white   red   rosé   sparkling
Name: _____
Vintage: _____
Varietal: _____
Price: _____

Body:	Simple	Moderately Complex	Complex
Acidity:	Low	Medium	High
Sweetness:	Dry	Off-dry	Sweet
Finish:	Short	Moderate	Long

Aromas & Flavors:

Whites/Roses

Citrus	Lemon, Grapefruit, Orange, Tangerine
Tree Fruit	Pear, Apple, Apricot, Peach, Nectarine
Tropical	Melon, Pineapple, Passion fruit, Banana, Mango
Floral	Geranium, Violet, Rose, Orange Blossom,
Herbal	Sage, Mint, Tea, Cut green grass
Mineral	Stone, Slate, Flint, Chalk
Spicy	Cinnamon, Nutmeg, Clove, Spiced Apple, Ginger
Nutty	Walnut, Almond, Hazelnut
Woody	Vanilla, Oak, Toast, Coconut
Yeast	Baked Bread, Bread Dough, Pie Crust
Caramel	Butter, Honey, Caramel, Butterscotch, Crème Brûlee
Other	Fuel/Diesel

Reds

Berry	Blackberry, Raspberry, Strawberry, Blueberry
Tree Fruit	Red Cherry, Black Cherry, Plum
Dried Fruit	Raisin, Fig, Prune, Berry Jam
Floral	Geranium, Violet, Rose
Herbal	Bell Pepper, Olive, Eucalyptus, Mint, Sage
Earth	Mushroom, Mineral, Forest floor
Meat	Smoked Meat, Bacon, Leather
Spice	Cinnamon, Clove, Black Pepper, Licorice/Anise
Woody	Vanilla, Oak, Cedar, Toast, Charred Wood, Tobacco
Caramel	Chocolate, Mocha, Molasses, Honey, Butterscotch
Other	Pencil Lead, Tar

Notes: _____
_____
_____

Rating

1	2	3	4	5
Don't Like It		It's Okay		I Love It!

...tell your friends at wineopolis.com

Sonoma Restaurants: A Guide

Naturally, it is time to move from talking about wine to talking about food. Sonoma has many incredible dining options and you will not want to miss the stand-out eateries and restaurants along the way. Again, we'll profile some gourmet restaurants as well as local hangouts so you have a variety of styles and prices to choose from. Below are our top 20 of the region. It's tough to whittle them down, but someone has to do it. And if you have a great suggestion or a new hidden gem, come tell us about it at Wineopolis.com.

Like the wineries, we will start our list with Sonoma and work our way north. We'll list the name, address and contact information, price, as well as a brief description of the menu and atmosphere.

PRICE GUIDE (for two entrees only):

$ - Less than $25
$$ - $26-35
$$$ - $36-50
$$$$ - $51 and up

Café La Haye

140 East Napa Street, Sonoma, CA 95476 / 707-935-5994
www.cafelahaye.com
Price: $$$
Hours: Dinner 5:30pm - 9pm Tuesday-Sunday
Reservations: Recommended

Café La Haye is located just off of the historic Sonoma plaza in Sonoma. This two-story eatery is always decorated with outstanding artwork (that changes seasonally) and has some artistic dishes as well, such as pan-seared quail with pomegranate vinaigrette and smoked trout crepes with caviar and crispy capers. This place is a favorite for those traveling up from San Francisco and given how many foodies there are in the Bay Area, you know it's good.

make notes in your Trip Log at the end of this section

The Red Grape

529 First Street West, Sonoma, CA 95474 / 707-996-4103
www.theredgrape.com
Price: $$
Hours: Lunch and Dinner daily from 11:30am - close
Reservations: Not needed

If you love pizza then you cannot miss out on The Red Grape. This pizza joint has over 30 kinds of pizza, from your general pepperoni to the unique roasted duck and gorgonzola pizza. You can choose your sauce (pesto, olive oil or tomato) and a wide variety of toppings. But they also have some non-pizza dishes such as fresh pastas, Panini sandwiches and salads. And there's a nice wine list so you won't miss out on tasting local labels.

Estate (Formerly Known As The General's Daughter)

400 West Spain Street, Sonoma, CA 95474 / 707-958-4004
www.thegeneralsdaughter.com
Price: $$$
Hours: Dinner Tuesday – Sunday 5:30pm to close
Reservations: Recommended

The General's Daughter provides upscale elegance with wine country charm. Housed in an old Victorian building, the restaurant offers mostly fixed price menus of three, four or five courses ranging from $50-$75 per person. They take pride in pairing local Sonoma wines with their gourmet foods and sometimes they have local winemakers who come by to talk about their wines during special winemaker dinners (in the summer months). You will definitely want to make a reservation.

The Girl & The Fig

110 West Spain Street, Sonoma, CA 95476 / 707-938-3634
www.thegirlandthefig.com
Price: $$$$
Hours: 11:30am – 10pm daily, Sunday brunch 10am, late night menu till 11pm Friday-Saturday
Reservations: Recommended

Along with its interesting name, The Girl & The Fig has some unique and delectable dishes accented by figs. Located on the ground floor of the Sonoma Hotel, this restaurant is awash in a sea of pastels and serves tasty dishes such as wild flounder meuneire. For cheese lovers, there are quite a few cheese and charcuterie plates that go perfect with local wines.

Share your experiences online at wineopolis.com

The Swiss Hotel

18 West Spain Street, Sonoma, CA 95476 / 707-938-2884
www.swisshotelsonoma.com
Price: $$$
Hours: Lunch 11:30am – 2:30pm, Dinner 5pm - close
Reservations: Not needed

This historic building was built back in the 1830s by General Mariano Vallejo's brother. Over the years, it has changed ownership and is now known as the Swiss Hotel. Besides offering a slice of Sonoma history, there's also a top-notch restaurant inside (though its cuisine is Italian, not Swiss). Here you can get scrumptious wood-fired pizzas and a wide selection of pastas. Besides the main dining room, there is also a very charming outdoor patio.

Glen Ellen Inn Oyster Grill & Martini Bar

13670 Arnold Drive, Glen Ellen, CA 95442 / 707-996-6409
www.glenelleninn.com
Price: $$$$
Hours: 11:30am – 9pm Friday-Tuesday, Dinner 5:30pm – 9pm Wednesday & Thursday
Reservations: Recommended

The restaurant at this Inn is set inside a small Cape Cod inspired cottage, where you can dine inside or outside on their porch and patio. They have oysters galore here, whether on the half shell, sautéed or fried. Beyond oysters, they serve many other California-inspired dishes which includes braised lamb shank and a smoked brie and spinach ravioli. When you want to unwind after a day of tasting or take a respite in the afternoon, this little cottage restaurant is ideal. The bar offers many wines but has dozens of martinis so make sure to try a cocktail.

Garden Court Café & Bakery

13647 Arnold Drive, Glen Ellen, CA 95442 / 707-935-1565
www.gardencourtcafe.com
Price: $
Hours: 8:30am – 2pm weekdays, 7:30am – 2pm weekends, closed Tuesdays
Reservations: Not needed

This is a popular local café known especially for breakfast. Locals love this place for its many variations on the popular Eggs Benedict dish and they have killer omelets! They're also open for lunch, offering many delicious soups, salads and sandwiches.

What did you eat?

Kenwood Restaurant

9900 Highway 12, Kenwood, CA 95452 / 707-833-6326
www.kenwoodrestaurant.com
Price: $$$$
Hours: 12pm – 9pm Wednesday-Saturday, 12pm – 8pm Sunday
Reservations: Recommended

Kenwood Restaurant was once voted one of the top 20 restaurants in the entire Bay Area by *Gourmet* magazine, so expect to be wowed by their cuisine. The menu has an abundance of fresh fish, meats and poultry choices, but make sure you leave room for dessert, and go for the flourless Swiss chocolate cake with raspberry coulis. They serve some of the best local Kenwood wines to accompany their menu dishes. You can watch the sunlight drift across scenic Sugarloaf Mountain and its surrounding vineyards if you are dining on the patio

Hana Japanese

101 Golf Course Drive, Rohnert Park, CA / 707-586-0270
www.hanajapanese.com
Price: $$$
Hours: Lunch 11:30am – 2:30pm Monday-Saturday, Dinner 5pm – 9pm Sunday-Thursday, and 5pm – 9:30pm Friday-Saturday
Reservations: Not needed

Just beyond the main drag in Sonoma is the community of Rohnert Park, east of Highway 101. If you're looking for good Japanese food (and good sushi) this is worth the trek. Hana Japanese is located in a strip mall, but don't let its humble appearance fool you. This is where the chef's eat; for good reason. Fresh fish (some flown in straight from Japan) are combined with the best local ingredients. Owner Ken Tominaga prides himself on exceptional combinations, such as unagi and foie gras. The sushi here is always fresh and the main courses are exceptional. Try the pan-seared thinly sliced Black Angus Rib-Eye Steak in a chili soy sauce. Yum.

Dierk's Parkside Café

404 Santa Rosa Avenue, Santa Rosa, CA 95404 / 707-573-5955
www.dierksparkside.com
Price: $$
Hours: 7am – 2pm daily
Reservations: Not accepted

Dierk's Parkside is a local eatery serving up unique dishes for breakfast and lunch every day. Chef Mark Dierkhising spent many years running upscale restaurants in Wine Country and now he brings that expertise to his food served in a casual café setting. Think of it as French comfort food without the

...tell your friends at wineopolis.com

pomp and circumstance. They use many fresh and locally grown ingredients, so it tastes good and is good for your health.

La Gare French Restaurant

208 Wilson Street, Santa Rosa, CA 95401 / 707-528-4355
www.lagarerestaurant.com
Price: $$$
Hours: Lunch & Dinner Wednesday-Sunday (Closed Monday & Tuesday)
Reservations: Recommended

La Gare is where you come when you want a quiet, romantic dinner for two. It's located in the historic Railroad Square in the city of Santa Rosa. In fact, La Gare is French for railway station. Being a local favorite, you'll want to reserve a table ahead of time. Expect to see many couples celebrating engagements, anniversaries and other special occasions. La Gare serves up country French cooking that would make Julia Child proud. They serve a wide selection of French wines (a rarity here) as well as local wines, so you'll have plenty of choices when looking to pair wine with your meal.

Stark's Steakhouse

521 Adams Street, Santa Rosa, CA 95401 / 707-546-5100
www.starkssteakhouse.com
Price: $$$$
Hours: 11:30am – 9pm Monday-Thursday, 11:30am – 10pm Friday, 5pm – 10pm Saturday, 5pm – 9pm Sunday
Reservations: Recommended

There aren't too many steakhouses in Sonoma, but we know a good one when we find it. Stark's Steakhouse has some of the best red meat around, so if you're a carnivore, definitely stop in for dinner. They cook up a great steak and offer many unique accompaniments such as foie gras, fried egg or blue cheese butter. This gem is in Santa Rosa, not far from Railroad Square.

Zazu Restaurant

3535 Guerneville Road, Santa Rosa, CA 95401 / 707-523-4814
www.zazurestaurant.com
Price: $$$
Hours: Dinner 5:30pm – close Wednesday-Sunday
Reservations: Recommended

Zazu is a roadhouse restaurant set amidst several wineries. So after a day of tasting, it's perfectly situated for you to hop on over and refuel your tank with some of your favorite down-home dishes. But if you're around Wednesday,

where did you go?

Thursday or Sunday night you can experience "Pinot and Pizza nights" where you can eat freshly baked pizza with a glass (or two) of Pinot Noir. Their main menu changes seasonally as they use a lot of fresh, locally grown ingredients (some grown on the owner's adjacent farm). But dessert is always a plus here, especially their dark chocolate fondue, so save room if you can.

Restaurant Mirepoix

275 Windsor River Road, Windsor, CA 95492 / 707-838-0162
www.restaurantmirepoix.com
Price: $$$
Hours: 11:30am – 9pm Tuesday-Saturday
Reservations: Recommended

In the heart of downtown Windsor is the Restaurant Mirepoix, which is a charming French style bistro. Mirepoix specializes in seasonal food paired with wine. In fact, they have a fixed-price menu of either four, five or six courses that's priced very reasonably, so it's the perfect affordable complement to your wine tasting odyssey. You can bet on the freshest seafood, as well as local meats and vegetables all done with a French twist. In the Spring and Summer months, we recommend eating out on their patio to take in the view.

Cyrus

29 North Street, Healdsburg, CA 95448 / 707-433-3311
www.cyrusrestaurant.com
Price: $$$$
Hours: Dinner 5:30pm – 9:30pm daily (Closed Tuesday and Wednesday during Winter)
Reservations: Required

If you've come to Sonoma to experience fine dining at its best, then you must eat at Cyrus. This elegant and upscale restaurant has a fixed price menu ranging from $70 to over $100 per person. But the price is worth it. The dishes are carefully selected and can be paired with wine to form a perfect tasting menu. The menu has strong French influences pairing fresh meats and vegetables with delectable sauces. Plan on dressing up and having a long, leisurely dinner here.

log it, blog it, share it at wineopolis.com

Bovolo

106 Matheson Street, Healdsburg, CA 95448 / 707-431-2962
www.bovolorestaurant.com
Price: $$
Hours: 9am – 8pm Sunday-Thursday, 9am – 9pm Friday-Saturday
Reservations: Not needed

Bovolo is a sister restaurant to Zazu from the same owners, John Stewart and Duskie Estes. Their slogan is "slow food…fast" which really just means you get fresh, hand-prepared meals without having to wait an eternity. The laid-back atmosphere only accentuates their creative cuisine. Our favorite is breakfast where you can enjoy a breakfast version of pasta carbonara as well as sweet and tangy goat cheese turnovers. They also serve lunch and dinner. They are well known for their artisan cured meats and fresh made bacon. They even serve bacon ice cream! They're located inside Copperfield's Books in Healdsburg Plaza.

Madrona Manor

1001 Westside Road, Healdsburg, CA 95448 / 707-433-4231
www.madronamanor.com
Price: $$$$
Hours: Dinner 6pm – 9pm Wednesday-Sunday
Reservations: Recommended

Madrona Manor is nestled among sprawling vineyards in an impressively ornate three-story mansion, which is also an Inn (we'll profile it later). The interior is opulent and lush, as if you're visiting European royalty. The dining room serves high-end California cuisine from chef Mallgren by candlelight. They have an á la carte as well as a tasting menu featuring some locally raised meat dishes such as lamb and rabbit, as well as fresh seafood. An extra special treat is the Madrona Manor Signature Cheese Course where you can taste cheeses from around the world.

Zin

344 Center Street, Healdsburg, CA 95448 / 707-473-0946
www.zinrestaurant.com
Price: $$$$
**Hours: Lunch 11:30am – 2pm Monday-Friday,
Dinner 5:30pm – close daily**
Reservations: Recommended

As you can probably guess from the title, this restaurant is inspired by the rich and fruity tones of Zinfandels. Pretty much most of the cuisine here is specially crafted to perfectly complement a glass of Zinfandel; which means

what did you see?

there are tons of Zinfandels to choose from on their wine list. The cuisine here is mostly American favorites, served with a twist. The menu changes seasonally, but look for favorites such as ribs, pork chops and chicken all served up with zesty sauces from local ingredients.

Applewood Inn & Restaurant

13555 Highway 116, Guerneville, CA / 800-555-8509
www.applewoodinn.com
Price: $$$$
Hours: Dinner Tuesday-Saturday
Reservations: Recommended

In the heart of Russian River Valley, tucked in a forest of majestic redwoods, is the charming Applewood Inn. Here you will find a restaurant housed in a private, fire-lit dining room just inside the main house. The food is a perfect blend of French and California cuisine with dishes such as crab profiterole with citrus salad or halibut with braised artichoke and mushroom ragoût. For dessert, try the chocolate ganache crêpe.

World Famous Hamburger Ranch And Pasta Farm

31195 N. Redwood Highway, Cloverdale, CA 95425 / 866-462-7421
www.worldfamoushamburgerranch.com
Price: $$
Hours: 7am – 9pm daily
Reservations: Not needed

Well, the name pretty much says it all. This local eatery in Cloverdale is down-home cooking done right. Yes, their hamburgers are spectacular. But, you can also choose from many other childhood favorites such as steak and barbecued chicken. They're open for breakfast, lunch and dinner and there's pretty much something for everyone on the menu here.

post your trip photos at wineopolis.com

Trip Log: Places to Eat

Restaurant: _____

Town: _____

Meal: Dinner   Lunch   Breakfast   Other

_____

Price: _____

What did you eat? _____

What did you like about it? _____

Notes: _____

_____

_____

_____

_____

_____

_____

_____

_____

_____

_____

_____

Rating

1	2	3	4	5
Don't Like It		It's Okay		I Love It!

bite, munch, blog, repeat

Trip Log: Places to Eat

Restaurant: _____

Town: _____

Meal: Dinner   Lunch   Breakfast   Other

                     _____

Price: _____

What did you eat?   _____

What did you like about it? _____

Notes: _____
_____
_____
_____
_____
_____
_____
_____
_____
_____
_____
_____

Rating

1	2	3	4	5
Don't Like It		It's Okay		I Love It!

Share your experiences online at wineopolis.com

Trip Log: Places to Eat

Restaurant: _____

Town: _____

Meal: Dinner   Lunch   Breakfast   Other

               _____

Price: _____

What did you eat? _____

What did you like about it? _____

Notes: _____

_____

_____

_____

_____

_____

_____

_____

_____

_____

_____

Rating

1	2	3	4	5
Don't Like It		It's Okay		I Love It!

let us know your favorites at wineopolis.com

Trip Log: Places to Eat

Restaurant: _____

Town: _____

Meal: Dinner   Lunch   Breakfast   Other

_____

Price: _____

What did you eat? _____

What did you like about it? _____

Notes: _____

_____

_____

_____

_____

_____

_____

_____

_____

_____

_____

Rating

1	2	3	4	5
Don't Like It		It's Okay		I Love It!

find free resources at wineopolis.com

Sonoma Activities Not to be Missed

Sonoma has many attractions *besides* wine tasting, so you'll just have to pencil in time to do some shopping, browsing and sightseeing. So get ready, now is our time to list the activities in Sonoma not to be missed. We will again go geographically, starting in the south and take you through the best sights, shops and events you need to see. But we're not all knowing, every experience is different and as a community we learn from each other's travels so be sure to share your trip with us at Wineopolis.com because we're always looking for new attractions to recommend.

Mystic Theatre & Music Hall

23 North Petaluma Blvd., Petaluma, CA / 707-765-2121
www.mystictheatre.com
Price: $15 - $30 per ticket (generally)

The Mystic Theatre & Music Hall is located in Petaluma, the first major city off Highway 101 when you enter Sonoma County. This venue has a lot of cool rock and roll acts, as well as the occasional stand-up comedian. What's just as fascinating as the musical acts is the building itself. Originally built in 1911, the building used to host vaudeville back in the day. The theatre has 500 seats, encompassing two levels. McNear's Saloon & Dining House is right next door, so it makes for a fun night out to catch a show and grab a bite or a drink.

The Olive Press

24724 Highway 121, Sonoma, CA 95476 / 800-965-4839
www.theolivepress.com
Hours: 10:30am – 5pm daily

This store prides itself for its award-winning California extra virgin olive oil and we agree. Here you can purchase their infamous oil AND taste up to six different oils at their tasting bar. After you're given their olive oil a try, you can walk on through to the Jacuzzi Family Winery and taste some wines. The store also has a selection of olive-themed pantry items and vinegars as well as gift baskets. Try the olive press tapenade and olive pasta sauce.

make notes in your Trip Log at the end of this section

California Missions Museum At Cline Cellars

24737 Highway 121, Sonoma, CA 95476 / 707-939-8051
www.californiamissionsmuseum.com
Price: Free
Hours: 10am – 4 pm daily

The State of California has some of the most well-preserved Spanish missions from its history with Spain and Mexico. Missions were built back when Spain tried to convert the local native Americans to Catholicism. Be sure to visit the museum here where you can witness perfectly scaled models of all 21 missions in the state of California. Nancy Cline, owner of Cline Cellars, bought the collection in 1998 and now has them on display in a building behind the Cline Cellars tasting room. Best of all, admission is free.

Historic Sonoma Plaza

Sonoma Plaza (between 1st and 2nd Streets), Sonoma, CA 95476

In the heart of Sonoma lies the historic Sonoma Plaza where the main attraction is the home of General Vallejo, who ruled the small village when the land was owned by Mexico. You can see his mansion and nearby barracks. Surrounding these historical buildings are many shops and restaurants. In the middle of the grounds is a great picnic spot covered by shade trees, a playground and duck pond. (There's an open container law so you can bring your wine with you when you picnic).

Spirits In Stone

452 First Street East, Sonoma, CA 95476 / 800-474-6624
www.spiritsinstone.com
401 Healdsburg Avenue, Healdsburg, CA 95448 / 877-774-6627
Hours: 10am – 6pm daily (Sonoma), 11am – 6pm Thursday-Sunday (Healdsburg)

Spirits In Stone houses a collection of Zimbabwe Shone sculpture. What's that you say? It's a new contemporary form of art out of Africa that uses simple stones as the inspiration to create evocative and imaginative shapes and designs. But words really can't do them justice; you need to come see for yourself. The store also contains a variety of African photographs and paintings as well as African-inspired music.

Tiddle E. Winks Vintage 5 & Dime

115 East Napa Street, Sonoma, CA 95476 / 707-939-6933
www.tiddleewinks.com
Hours: 11am – 5pm Sunday-Tuesday, 11am-6pm Wednesday-Thursday, 10am-6pm Friday-Saturday

Take one step into this store and you'll step back into your childhood. Tiddle E. Winks is a vintage five-and-dime that covers decades worth of Americana from toys, games, candies and collectibles. You're more than likely to find whatever nostalgic toy you cherished from your childhood here or even be inspired to buy some vintage lunch boxes or retro signs. Come here to be a child again, if only for an hour or two.

Vella Cheese Company

315 Second Street East, Sonoma, CA 95476 / 800-848-0505
www.vellacheese.com
Hours: 9:30am – 6pm Monday-Saturday

The Vella Cheese Company has been selling handmade cheeses since 1931, yet the stone building they operate in has been standing since 1905! You will find some of the best cheeses in the world made here. They're simply scrumptious and the perfect complement to all the local wines you'll be tasting. Be sure to try their award-winning Special Select Dry Jack and Romanello Dulce as well as their sharp raw milk cheddar.

Train Town

20264 Broadway, Sonoma, CA 95476 / 707-938-3912
www.traintown.com
Price: Admission to park is free, train ride is $3-$4 per person
Hours: 10am – 5pm Friday-Sunday (September-May), Daily (June-August)

Train Town is "the most well-developed scale railroad in the Americas!" This place features a miniature train that children and adults alike can ride and enjoy. The train travels through a beautifully landscaped park filled with native trees and animals, bridges, tunnels, waterfalls, and many replicas of local historic buildings. Outside the train ride, there's a fully restored vintage carousel as well as other theme park rides such as a Ferris Wheel and roller coaster. This place is perfect for those coming to Sonoma with families.

what else did you do?

Sonoma Valley Museum Of Art

551 Broadway, Sonoma, CA 95476 / 707-939-7862
www.svma.org
Price: $5 per person, $8 for families
Hours: 11am - 5pm Wednesday-Sunday

The Sonoma Valley Museum of Art is a small museum yet it has exhibited some interesting collections from California and across the U.S. including drawings, paintings, photography, sculptures, pottery, textiles, woodwork and even toys. They feature the work of local artists as well as national and international artists. The museum store is a treat and has some great art books, coffee table books and cookbooks. This is the perfect place to come cool your heels for a few hours in the afternoon.

Avalon Players Shakespeare Company

Gundlach Bundschu Winery, Sonoma, CA / 707-996-3264
www.sonomashakespeare.com
Price: $20 for adults, $10 for children under 12

Since 1980, this local company has been performing Shakespeare to Wine Country visitors (during the summer months) on the luscious lawn at Gundlach Bundschu Winery. It's the perfect opportunity to pack a picnic lunch (complete with wine), sprawl out and take in a little culture. Seating for the show is either on picnic tables (first-come first-served basis) or simply on the lawn. If you didn't bring wine, don't worry. You can get some in the winery tasting room. Check the website for dates and show times.

Jack London State Historic Park

2400 London Ranch Road (off Arnold Drive), Glen Ellen, CA 95442 / 707-938-5216
www.jacklondonpark.com
Price: $8 per car
Hours: Daily 10am - 5pm

This park is located on the grounds once owned by famous local novelist Jack London. He called it Beauty Ranch. His goal was not only to preserve the beauty of the landscape, but to experiment with new technologically advanced methods of ranching. Today on the property is a museum called the "Wolf House" ruin (a stone mansion where he hoped to live when complete), the Winery Ruin as well as barns and silos back from his time spent on the ranch. There's also the farmhouse where he lived and wrote until he died. Surrounding the buildings is almost seven miles of trails for hiking, biking and horse riding. It's worth a short visit or an entire afternoon if you have the time.

...tell your friends at wineopolis.com

Wine Country Chocolates

14301 Arnold Drive, Glen Ellen, CA 95442 / 707-938-9911
www.winecountrychocolates.com
Hours: 10am – 5pm daily

Another great pairing for wine is chocolate, so don't miss out on tasting (and buying) some of the best locally made chocolates. Wine Country Chocolates is a mother and daughter operation that specializes in delectable truffles made with local wine. Whether it's Zinfandel, Cabernet Sauvignon or a sparkling white wine, these truffles will melt in your mouth. They also have a wide selection of fruit-infused truffles, using the best locally grown fruits, of course. Be sure to come in and belly up to the bar at their "chocolate tasting room" and then leave with a box (or two).

Charles M. Schulz Museum And Research Center

2301 Hardies Lane, Santa Rosa, CA 95403 / 707-579-4452
www.schulzmuseum.org
Price: Admission to museum is $10 adults, $5 for children and seniors
Hours: Weekdays 11 am to 5 pm, Weekends 10 am to 5 pm (Closed Tuesdays in Winter)

This museum is dedicated to the life and works of cartoonist Charles M. Schultz; a Santa Rosa resident until his death in 2000. His unforgettable *Peanuts* characters will live on for many years to come. The museum houses work from his long 50-year plus career and houses an archive and research library for students, scholars and other budding cartoonists. (There are classrooms on site where they have workshops and special classes). In the museum store, you can find everything *Snoopy* and *Peanuts* that your heart can possibly desire.

Snoopy's Gallery And Gift Shop

1665 West Steele Lane, Santa Rosa, CA 95403 / 800-959-3385
www.snoopygift.com
Hours: 10am – 6pm daily

Since you're already in a *Peanuts* frame of mind after visiting the Charles M. Schulz Museum, you should naturally hop on over to the nearby Snoopy's Gallery and Gift Shop. Here you will find everything *Snoopy* in the gift shop, and the adjacent gallery contains many awards, drawings and personal memorabilia from cartoonist Charles Schulz himself. Afterwards you can go next door and ice skate at the Empire Ice Arena.

what did you see?

Getaway Adventures

2228 Northpoint Parkway, Santa Rosa, CA 95407 / 800-499-2453
www.getawayadventures.com
Price: $125-$145 depending on tour

At Getaway Adventures you can tour a winery by bike or a kayak down part of the Russian River. Their winery bike tour (cleverly called a Sip and Cycle tour) is a great way to visit a handful of wineries, see the landscape and enjoy a catered lunch. (Service is also offered in Napa.) This will put you near the Healdsburg area, which has some fantastic wineries. If you're looking for a little more adventure, you can take a kayak tour. The river is pretty mellow and you'll pass some of the best lands in Sonoma County. Check out their website for all prices, promotions, and tour offerings.

Safari West

3115 Porter Creek Road, Santa Rosa, CA 95404 / 707-579-2551
www.safariwest.com
Price: Varies (but a basic tour is around $65 for adults, $30 for children)

Bet you didn't think you could get an African safari experience in wine country, but you can. This Safari park is worthy of the label, thankfully. Located on a private reserve, Safari West spans nearly 400 acres and is home to many exotic mammals and birds. This isn't your typical drive-through animal park or even a zoo. Safari West is a true excursion. It's a wildlife preserve where you can get up close and personal with the animals, learn about preservation and conservation, and the propagation of endangered species. Come see these animals in their natural habitat (and stay the night, if you can, in one of their cozy cottages).

Jimtown Store

6706 Highway 128, Healdsburg, CA 95448 / 707-433-1212
www.jimtown.com
Hours: 7am – 5pm Monday-Friday, 7:30am – 5pm Saturday-Sunday

Jimtown Store is a true authentic country store owned by local artist Carrie Brown and her husband Jim (hence the name). Inside, you'll find a slew of antiques and folk art and can even sit down for a hearty meal capped with a great cup of coffee. The building itself has a long history of being a general store and was built over 100 years ago. The café has some classic American dishes like chili and chicken soup made from local ingredients and they have a very wide selection of vegetarian dishes (so they're healthy, too). Carrie makes a line of tasty homemade condiments such as a fig & olive spread, so be sure to check out her collection.

post your trip photos at wineopolis.com

Flying Horse Carriage Tours

Alexander Valley Vineyards, 8644 Highway 128, Healdsburg, CA 95448 / 707-849-8989
www.flyinghorse.org
Price: $145 per person (includes tasting fees)

Available at the Alexander Valley Vineyards (one of our recommendations) is a horse-drawn carriage ride. Romantic and a great way to leisurely tour the vineyards. The carriage ride also includes a gourmet lunch and as an added bonus, the carriage ride stops at a few *other* wineries so you can try a few tastings. The entire tour takes about four hours and is well worth the time. What better way to drink wine and experience Sonoma than by horse-drawn carriage. The tour begins at 12:30pm.

Vignettes

110 Matheson Street, Healdsburg, CA 95448 / 707-433-6243
www.vignetteshealdsburg.com
Hours: 11am – 6pm daily

Vignettes is part art gallery, part gift shop and it is here where you will find a wide selection of art to fit almost any taste: jewelry, wire sculptures, photographs, paintings, watercolors, pottery, ceramics, etc. Vignettes also showcase some local artists, including multi-plate etchings from artist Gail Packer and watercolors by Douglas Chun.

play, shop, blog, repeat

River Rock Casino

3250 Highway 128, Geyserville, CA 95441 / 707-857-2777
www.riverrockcasino.com
Price: Free (well, until you gamble)

We can't talk about attractions without mentioning a casino! Though we're not in Vegas, California does have some worthy casinos, owned by different Native American Tribes. In Geyserville, you'll find the River Rock Casino. Besides the gambling tables and slot machines, there's a restaurant and some gift shops where you can get local souvenirs as well as Native American artifacts. If you're feeling lucky, come give it a try.

Share your experiences online at wineopolis.com

Trip Log: Things to See & Do

Name: _____

Town: _____

Category: Recreation   Shopping   Museum   Music   Culture   Family

Price: _____

What did you like about it? _____

_____

Notes: _____

_____
_____
_____
_____
_____
_____
_____
_____
_____
_____
_____
_____

Rating

1	2	3	4	5
Don't Like It		It's Okay		I Love It!

log it, blog it, share it at wineopolis.com

Trip Log: Things to See & Do

Name: _____

Town: _____

Category: Recreation   Shopping   Museum   Music   Culture   Family

Price: _____

What did you like about it? _____

_____

Notes: _____

_____
_____
_____
_____
_____
_____
_____
_____
_____
_____
_____
_____

Rating

1	2	3	4	5
Don't Like It		It's Okay		I Love It!

let us know your favorites at wineopolis.com

Trip Log: Things to See & Do

Name: _____

Town: _____

Category: Recreation   Shopping   Museum   Music   Culture   Family

Price: _____

What did you like about it? _____

_____

Notes: _____

_____

_____

_____

_____

_____

_____

_____

_____

_____

_____

_____

Rating

1	2	3	4	5
Don't Like It		It's Okay		I Love It!

find free resources at wineopolis.com

Trip Log: Things to See & Do

Name: _____

Town: _____

Category: Recreation   Shopping   Museum   Music   Culture   Family

Price: _____

What did you like about it? _____

_____

Notes: _____

_____

_____

_____

_____

_____

_____

_____

_____

_____

_____

_____

Rating

1	2	3	4	5
Don't Like It		It's Okay		I Love It!

Share your experiences online at wineopolis.com

Where to Stay in Sonoma

Now it is time to rest your weary head. Here are some of the fabulous places you can stay during your trip! In the following pages, we outline some of our favorite. We'll encompass a variety so as to fit all tastes, including hotels, motels, resorts, and bed & breakfasts. We'll list the chains you know, as well as some locally owned gems. For us, comfort is king, as you need to be well rested to enjoy all that wine. Be sure to record your stay and come tell us about it at Wineopolis.com!

Again, we will start our list with Sonoma and work our way north up the valley. We'll list the name, address and contact information, price, location, as well as a description of the amenities you can expect.

Note on prices: Hotel rates vary by season and occasion, so we will give a price range according to their listed regular rates during the high season months. It is best to always check the hotel website for your specific dates to see what rates and specials apply.

PRICE GUIDE (per night based on double occupancy):

$ - Less than $100
$$ - $101 to $175
$$$ - $176 to $250
$$$$ - More than $251

El Dorado Hotel

405 First Street West, Sonoma, CA 95476 / 800-289-3031
www.eldoradosonoma.com
Price: $$$ - $$$$

The El Dorado Hotel is a boutique hotel with 27 elegant rooms (four of them, bungalows), located just off of Sonoma's historic plaza square. In addition to being within walking distance from all the plaza shops and restaurants, this hotel has its own upscale eatery (El Dorado Kitchen) as well as a small café and solar-heated pool. The building was originally built in the 1840s by General Vallejo's brother Salvador and previously served as a government office and even a winery. There are some rooms with balconies facing the plaza, so be sure to ask for a room with a view.

Share your experiences online at wineopolis.com

Ledson Hotel

480 First Street East, Sonoma, CA 95476 / 707-996-9779
www.ledsonhotel.com
Price: $$$$

On the other side of the plaza, lies the small but stately Ledson Hotel. This hotel is owned by the Ledson Winery. Upstairs are six guestrooms, all with whirlpool tubs, fireplaces and balconies. Downstairs is a wine bar called Harmony Lounge, that offers quality Ledson wines paired with different small-plate entrees, cheese plates and antipasto. Enjoy them inside by the fire or outside at a sidewalk table. The building itself looks like a historic Spanish mission, so it's also a great photo opportunity and a luxurious place to stay.

Sonoma Hotel

110 West Spain Street, Sonoma, CA 95476 / 800-468-6016
www.sonomahotel.com
Price: $$ - $$$

This hotel is located in the northwestern part of Sonoma Plaza and dates back to the 1880s when it was originally the town hall. Nowadays, the Sonoma Hotel is filled with a variety of American antiques from the 19th century and each room is given its own distinct name and personality. The best is perhaps the Vallejo Room (named after the General) with its carved rosewood furniture once owned by the family. The lobby boasts a large stone fireplace and Italian stained glass. Don't let all the antiques fool you, as every room is decidedly modern with a private bath, as well as all the amenities you'd expect from a modern-day hotel. BTW: This hotel is the home to our recommended restaurant The Girl & The Fig.

Best Western Sonoma Valley Inn

550 Second Street West, Sonoma, CA 95476 / 800-334-5784
www.sonomavalleyinn.com
Price: $$$

Sonoma Valley Inn is an upscale offering under the Best Western umbrella. It's not in a centuries-old building like some of the other local hotels (this was built in the late 1980s) but it is charming nonetheless. The building is Spanish mission-style, which gives it a historic ambiance. But most importantly, the Inn is walking distance from the plaza and all the local shops and restaurants you'll want to visit. There is a spa onsite and rates include a free continental breakfast that can be delivered to your room. It's also much bigger than some other local hotels (73 rooms) and it comes with some perks (children under 16 stay for free and even dogs are allowed for a fee).

make notes in your Trip Log at the end of this section

Gaige House

13540 Arnold Drive, Glen Ellen, CA 95442 / 800-935-0237
www.gaige.com
Price: $$$$

It can be said that Gaige House is perfectly Zen – this Asian-inspired boutique luxury hotel is perfectly nestled in the heart of southern Sonoma County Wine Country. Gaige House rests on three acres and has 23 guestrooms and suites. Eight of the suites have granite soak tubs along with an outside private Japanese garden. When you're looking for peace, serenity and opulence, look no further than Gaige House. There's also on on-site swimming pool, Jacuzzi, as well as a spa. For an extra cost, you can enjoy a two or three course breakfast so you can fill up before a long day of wine tasting, though they do not serve lunch or dinner.

Beltane Ranch

11775 Highway 12, Glen Ellen, CA 95442 / 707-996-6501
www.beltaneranch.com
Price: $$$

When you visit Beltane Ranch, you are taking a step back into Sonoma Valley's history Surrounded by some of the most beautiful vineyards, orchards and gardens, this 1892 ranch house and adjoining cottage looks like it stepped right out of a painting. There are many walking trails that take you out into the countryside, past grazing horses and cattle, an olive orchard, and an organic garden where you can see the fresh produce being picked for your next meal. There are five guest rooms inside the ranch house and a private cottage. All rooms have private baths and outdoor entrances. Breakfast is served every morning in the dining room or on the porch outside your room. This place is very affordable but also very popular, so book early!

The Kenwood Inn & Spa

10400 Highway 12, Kenwood, CA 95452 / 800-353-6966
www.kenwoodinn.com
Price: $$$$

If you've come to Wine Country for relaxation, opulence, and pampering as well as wine tasting, then you should really consider staying at the Kenwood Inn & Spa. This treasure, located in the heart of Southern Sonoma Wine Country, is intimate, personalized, peaceful and serene. The Inn itself is on a secluded hillside amongst many vineyards. There are only 30 rooms, each with carefully selected antiques and luxury fabrics, as well as a private spa-like bath and fireplace. There's a full-service spa offering pretty much every service under the sun. During your stay, you can have breakfast in the dining

room or on outdoor tables and in the evening, the on-site wine bar offers food and drinks. It's expensive (upwards of $500) but well worth it when you want to treat yourself.

Hyatt Vineyard Creek Hotel, Spa & Conference Center

170 Railroad Street, Santa Rosa, CA 95401 / 707-284-1234
www.vineyardcreek.hyatt.com
Price: $$$$

This Hyatt Hotel is conveniently located in downtown Santa Rosa, so it's close by the local shops and restaurants, as well as a short drive away from a whole host of wineries. This resort is reminiscent of a Tuscan villa and has 155 rooms as well as many upscale amenities desired by vacationers and business travelers alike. The hotel has a fine dining restaurant, wine bar and café, as well as lush grounds filled with lavender, wisteria and roses. Let us not forget the fitness center, spa and steam room. This resort has it all.

The Gables Inn

4257 Petaluma Hill Road, Santa Rosa, CA 95404 / 800-422-5376
www.thegablesinn.com
Price: $$$ - $$$$

This beautiful candy-pink Victorian house was originally constructed in 1877 at the height of Victorian Gothic architecture in America. The name Gables Inn comes from the 15 gables that dominate the shape of the house. Nowadays, it's a charming bed & breakfast with seven guestrooms (two handicapped accessible) and a private cottage. The house sits on three acres and has some great views across the valley. What is truly a standout with this B&B is the home-cooked breakfast that is served on site and includes coffee, fresh squeezed juice, home baked breads and a hearty entrée.

Melitta Station Inn

5850 Melita Road, Santa Rosa, CA 95409 / 800-504-3099
www.melittastationinn.com
Price: $$$ - $$$$

Melitta Station Inn is a bed & breakfast and spa. The name comes from the fact that it was once a railway station and some evidence to that still exists in the architecture. Today, the Inn has a subtle European ambiance and houses six guest rooms, including one suite. At the spa, you can enjoy a complimentary soak in the hot tub and/or a massage (for an additional charge). Breakfast is served every morning and starts with fresh fruit and

where did you stay?

then either a sweet or savory entrée. Though not as ornate as some other B&Bs, it is clean, comfortable and the people here are very friendly.

Vintners Inn

4350 Barnes Road, Santa Rosa, CA 95403 / 800-421-2584
www.vintnersinn.com
Price: $$$$

Vintners Inn claims they are Wine Country and we're not going to disagree. This charming Inn located just outside of Santa Rosa looks like a French country estate complete with arched windows and wrought-iron balcony railings. Each room here (all 44 of them) are a complete oasis with private fireplace and luxury bath. Outside, the view has rolling vineyards, landscaped gardens and a courtyard complete with fountain. There's a great restaurant nearby (John Ash & Co.) and every morning here begins with breakfast either inside the dining room or out on the terrace. There's also an outdoor whirlpool spa, perfect for soaking under the stars.

Grape Leaf Inn

539 Johnson Street, Healdsburg, CA 95448 / 707-433-8140
www.grapeleafinn.com
Price: $$$$

You'll find the Grape Leaf Inn in a beautiful Queen Anne Victorian house from the turn of the last century. The 12 guestrooms and three guest cottages are all very different in look and feel and can fit just about any taste, from modern to country rustic, to super girlish pink. And, there's a daily gourmet breakfast as well. Be sure to take a walk through the many award-winning gardens that surround the property, especially the English rose garden. But what really stands out about the Grape Leaf is they have a private wine cellar they call the "Speakeasy" which you can only enter by a secret bookcase entry. Here you can taste some great local wines along with fresh artisan bread.

Hotel Healdsburg

25 Matheson Street, Healdsburg, CA 95448 / 800-889-7188
www.hotelhealdsburg.com
Price: $$$$

The Hotel Healdsburg is located right on Healdsburg's historic Town Plaza. Although relatively new (it opened only a few years ago) it is already a top-rated hotel and very popular with travelers (translation: book early). The hotel has a full-service spa, pool, fitness center, landscaped country garden and Charlie Palmer's Dry Creek Kitchen. Included is a daily breakfast served

...tell your friends at wineopolis.com

in the lobby from 6am – 10am. The rooms are upscale yet comfortable and the bathrooms have a large soak tub and walk-in showers. Best of all, most rooms have a private balcony where you can take in the sights and sounds of historic Healdsburg.

Healdsburg Inn On The Plaza

110 Matheson Street, Healdsburg, CA 95448 / 800-431-8663
www.healdsburginn.com
Price: $$$$

This place is larger than most bed & breakfasts and is both chic and rustic. It is perfectly situated in the historic Healdsburg plaza. The rooms (totaling 12) all have private baths and most have their own fireplaces. The Carriage House is behind the main building and the rooms here have a private balcony. On the second floor is a solarium where breakfast is served each morning and in the afternoon they offer complimentary wine, tea and hors d'oeuvres. There are additional services available for a price such as breakfast delivered to your room and in-room spa services.

Madrona Manor

1001 Westside Road, Healdsburg, CA 95448 / 800-258-4003
www.madronamanor.com
Price: $$$$

This estate is off the beaten path in lovely Dry Creek Valley, though it is still near enough to Healdsburg to enjoy the shopping. The fantastic manor was built back in 1880 and has 21 rooms (some with fireplaces, others with balconies) amongst four buildings set on grounds that are a mixture of landscaped gardens and dense forests. There is a stellar restaurant on-site (profiled in the Restaurant section) if you want an elegant dinner and there's a complimentary gourmet buffet breakfast served each morning for guests. This is another popular place for weddings, so book well in advance if traveling here in the summer months.

Best Western Dry Creek Inn

198 Dry Creek Road, Healdsburg, CA 95448 / 800-222-5784
www.drycreekinn.com
Price: $$ - $$$

Another Best Western offering, the Dry Creek Inn is a simple, clean motel whose real draw is that it is perfectly situated among the best wineries in Dry Creek Valley and is only five minutes from downtown Healdsburg. The main building has 103 rooms, all clean and neat with private baths and modern

sleep, shower, blog, repeat

amenities. A newer Tuscan building has 60 rooms and these are a bit more upscale (in-room fireplaces). So you can choose whatever fits your pleasure (and your budget). A complimentary continental breakfast is included and there's an on-site pool and whirlpool. When you've come to explore wineries, and not stay in your hotel room, then this place is ideal.

Sebastopol Inn

6751 Sebastopol Avenue, Sebastopol, CA / 800-653-1082
www.sebastopolinn.com
Price: $$ - $$$

In the middle of the Russian River Valley in the small town of Sebastopol is the Sebastopol Inn. Located near the quaint downtown area and several shops and eateries, this charming Inn has comfortable rooms, as well as an on-site day spa, heated pool and Jacuzzi. There's also a charming garden, courtyard and fountain. There are a few suites with a spa tub and fireplace if you're looking to upgrade. If you're hungry, you can enjoy nearby Coffee Catz Coffeehouse, which has live entertainment at night and a Sunday Jazz brunch.

Hope-Bosworth House

21238 Geyserville Avenue, Geyserville, CA 95441 / 800-825-4233
www.hope-inns.com
Price: $$$$

The Hope-Bosworth House is another immaculately restored Victorian B&B that is surrounded by a picket fence covered in elegant roses. There are only four guestrooms here, but they are beautifully appointed with antiques and hand-made furniture from America's past. In the dining room each morning, breakfast is served with a selection of fresh-baked bread and pastries along with a main egg dish. A sister house, the Hope-Merrill House is just across the street so you have your pick of country elegance along Geyserville Avenue.

Share your experiences online at wineopolis.com

Old Crocker Inn

1126 Old Crocker Inn Road, Cloverdale, CA 95425 / 800-716-2007
www.oldcrockerinn.com
Price: $$$ - $$$$

The Old Crocker Inn is perfectly tucked into a hillside outside of Cloverdale in the northern part of Sonoma County. The Inn was originally the hunting retreat for railroad magnate Charles Crocker in the late 1800s and now serves as a rustic B&B for those wanting to stay outside the main drag in Sonoma. All guest rooms and suites have a private bath and private entry whether in the main lodge or adjacent cabins. There's a full breakfast every morning. You can take a swim in the outdoor pool or opt for an in-room massage. Tough choices to make, but no matter what you do here, you'll leave relaxed.

Vintage Towers Inn

302 North Main Street, Cloverdale, CA / 888-886-9377
www.vintagetowers.com
Price: $$$ - $$$$

If you're looking for a bed & breakfast in Cloverdale, then look to Vintage Towers Inn. This charming country-inspired B&B has some unusually shaped towers, one is circular, one is square and one is octagonal – making it a standout amongst the neighborhood. There are seven guestrooms, but you'll want to stay in one of the tower suites. They all have a sitting area, sleeping area and private bath as well as some great views from the rooms' windows. There is a charming dining room as well as two sitting parlors where you can kick up your feet. After a long day of wine tasting, there are plenty of outdoor spaces around the Inn where you can relax from the porch swing on the front veranda, to the fire pit surrounded by rose bush trellises. Room rates vary depending on the room and season, so check their website for more information.

log it, blog it, share it at wineopolis.com

Trip Log: Places to Stay

Name: _____

Town: _____

Type: Hotel   Motel   Resort   B&B

_____

Price: _____

What amenities did they have? _____

_____

Spa   Breakfast   Dining   Internet/WiFi   Room Service   Pool/Jacuzzi   Parking

What did you like about it? _____

_____

Notes: _____

_____
_____
_____
_____
_____
_____
_____
_____
_____
_____
_____

Rating

1	2	3	4	5
Don't Like It		It's Okay		I Love It!

post your trip photos at wineopolis.com

Trip Log: Places to Stay

Name: _____

Town: _____

Type: Hotel   Motel   Resort   B&B

_____

Price: _____

What amenities did they have? _____

_____

Spa   Breakfast   Dining   Internet/WiFi   Room Service   Pool/Jacuzzi   Parking

What did you like about it? _____

_____

Notes: _____

_____
_____
_____
_____
_____
_____
_____
_____
_____
_____
_____

Rating

1	2	3	4	5
Don't Like It		It's Okay		I Love It!

let us know your favorites at wineopolis.com

Trip Log: Places to Stay

Name: _____

Town: _____

Type: Hotel   Motel   Resort   B&B

_____

Price: _____

What amenities did they have? _____

_____

Spa   Breakfast   Dining   Internet/WiFi   Room Service   Pool/Jacuzzi   Parking

What did you like about it? _____

_____

Notes: _____

_____
_____
_____
_____
_____
_____
_____
_____
_____
_____
_____

Rating

1	2	3	4	5
Don't Like It		It's Okay		I Love It!

find free resources at wineopolis.com

Trip Log: Places to Stay

Name: _____

Town: _____

Type: Hotel   Motel   Resort   B&B

_____

Price: _____

What amenities did they have? _____

Spa   Breakfast   Dining   Internet/WiFi   Room Service   Pool/Jacuzzi   Parking

What did you like about it? _____

_____

Notes: _____

_____
_____
_____
_____
_____
_____
_____
_____
_____
_____
_____

Rating

1	2	3	4	5
Don't Like It		It's Okay		I Love It!

Share your experiences online at wineopolis.com

SHARE YOUR JOURNEY!

Keep in mind that the members of Wineopolis are gathered together to learn from each other's experiences. Keep track of your tasting notes, reviews, excursions as well as any photos. By keeping notes on your Sonoma getaway, you can enlighten the rest of us!

Share your experiences online at wineopolis.com

V. GETTING AROUND & OTHER IMPORTANT STUFF

Hopefully, you are now super excited about traveling to the Northern California Wine Country. But before you head out the door, we need to talk about some transportation options, as well as some other practical information. Because Napa and Sonoma are closer to country living than city living, you'll need to research options as far as how to get there, and how to get around *once* you are there. We've done the work for you. As always, if there's something we've missed or you'd like to share how you go out and about in Napa and Sonoma, please come share it with us at www.wineopolis.com. But for now, take a browse for some transportation options, as well as other safety precautions you'll want to take.

Travel by Air, Train and Auto

You have some options for how you get to Napa and Sonoma. For most, it will require a series of journeys, not just one continuous plane ride. We'll break down the modes of transportation into both Napa and Sonoma.

Traveling by Air

There are three major airports nearby to both Napa and Sonoma and they are located in San Francisco, Oakland and Sacramento. There's also a commercial regional airport in Sonoma, with many smaller airports for private planes in both Napa and Sonoma County. Your best bet will be to fly to a major airport nearby then either rent a car, take an airport shuttle, or try to connect to the regional airport in Sonoma. We'll list your options below.

San Francisco International Airport (SFO)

San Francisco, California / 800-435-9736
www.flysfo.com

San Francisco International is an enormous airport located a few miles south of downtown San Francisco. Almost all major and minor airline carriers service here. There are also several rental car outlets as well as shuttles to area hotels.

Oakland International Airport (OAK)

Oakland, California / 510-563-3300
www.flyoakland.com
www.oaklandairport.com

Oakland is a large city across the bay from San Francisco and is geographically a little closer to both Sonoma and Napa. It is also a smaller airport, which makes for easier traveling. You will find many major airlines here as well as some regional ones that may connect to the smaller regional airport up north.

Sacramento International Airport (SMF)

Sacramento, California / 916-929-5411
www.sacairports.org

This airport has been growing in recent years and has a large list of national carriers that service the airport. There are also several rental car companies on site. Sacramento lies directly east of Sonoma and Napa Counties in the valley over the mountains, which will make your driving route a bit jagged. Try to connect from here to a smaller regional airport if you can.

Charles M. Schulz-Sonoma County Airport

Santa Rosa, California (Sonoma) / 707-565-7240
www.sonomacountyairport.com

This is the biggest regional airport in Sonoma County, located in Santa Rosa towards the middle of the valley. There has been a recent multi-million dollar

Share your experiences online at wineopolis.com

upgrade to the airport, so it's a great option when looking to fly directly to the region. They have daily connection flights through Horizon Air out of Los Angeles International Airport (LAX) as well as Las Vegas, Seattle, and Portland, so you may find your best connection out of one of those airports. There are also a handful of rental car companies on site if you are planning on continuing on to another part of the Valley.

Napa County Airport

Napa, California (Napa) / 707-253-4300
www.napacountyairport.org

Napa County Airport is the largest regional airport in Napa County (and that's not saying much). It is located in the town of Napa on the southern end of the valley. It is called "The Skyport to Wine Country" and it has plenty of charm, though there are no commercial flights available here, only charter flights.

Evans Airport Service (Napa)

4075 Solano Avenue, Napa, CA 94558 / 707-255-1559
www.evanstransportation.com

Evans Airport Service operates shuttle vans that service the town of Napa from both San Francisco International Airport and Oakland International (both ways). They run eight departures daily between SFO and five between OAK. The fare from the airport to the terminal in Napa is $29 per person (kids under 13 are half price). They will also take you directly to some of the local hotels and resorts for $49 per person. You will need to check their website for locations that are serviced. From their terminal location you can also look into several charter buses and wine tours.

Sonoma County Airport Express (Sonoma)

5807 Old Redwood Highway, Santa Rosa, CA 95403 / 800-327-2024
www.airportexpressinc.com

This is another shuttle van service between Santa Rosa in Sonoma County, and both airports in San Francisco and Oakland. They have 15 daily runs between SFO and 10 between OAK. A one-way fare costs $30 per person (kids under 12 are free). There are three stops along the way: The Petaluma Fairgrounds in Petaluma, the DoubleTree Hotel in Rohnert Park, and the Days Inn on Santa Rosa Avenue. Otherwise, you'll arrive at the main terminal in Santa Rosa.

Traveling by Train or Bus

We know trains aren't necessarily a popular way to travel, but they're so cool! California has the Amtrak which makes for a very scenic and comfortable trip. But if trains aren't your thing, there is always the reliable Greyhound Bus Line. Info for both is below.

Amtrak

Martinez, California / 800-872-7245
www.amtrak.com

The Amtrak actually only goes as far as Martinez which is about 30 miles south of Napa. However, from there you can take a bus to many Napa and Sonoma cities, and then take a bus back to the Martinez station for your return trip. The Amtrak train has major stops in Oakland and San Jose, so if you fly into either of those cities you are in luck. But even better, the Martinez station can connect you to almost anywhere else in California or the county that you'd like to go. Check out their website for a list of destinations that the train services.

Greyhound Bus Lines

435 Santa Rosa Avenue, Santa Rosa, CA / 800-231-2222
www.greyhound.com

Greyhound has been around forever, but lucky for us they just overhauled their image. The buses are much more modern and comfortable, and it makes for a great way to travel to Wine Country if you're in the mood to take a long, scenic trip. The main stop is in Santa Rosa in Sonoma County. There are smaller stops to be had in Napa, Sonoma and Petaluma, but you'll need to contact them for drop-off and pick-up info.

Traveling by Auto

Traveling to Wine Country by car is always a convenient option. For one, you'll get to see the sights of the road. Secondly, you'll have a way to get around the rest of the valley once you're here. We don't have the time or space to go through *every* route that leads in and out of the area, but we'll highlight the main arteries that get you to Napa and Sonoma and those in-between.

Note: There is a law in California that prohibits a driver from talking on a cell phone while driving. The penalty is steep - a few hundred dollars - so don't even think about taking that chance. Use a hands-free option or don't use it at all.

US HIGHWAY 101 (North-South)

This major highway, locally called the Redwood Highway, is the main drag north and south through most of California. You will drive straight through Sonoma County and hit all the major cities (Petaluma, Santa Rosa, Healdsburg, and Cloverdale). Travel will be slower when you pass through bigger cities and make sure to check the speed limit as it tends to drop when within city limits. When you're coming from San Francisco or south, this is the best way to get into Sonoma or to connect with another highway to get to Napa.

HIGHWAY 1 (North-South)

Highway 1 is its own scenic attraction. It's the coastal highway that stretches up the coastline from San Diego all the way up to Oregon. The most scenic stretch is probably south of San Francisco along Big Sur, but there's also a very dramatic stretch along the coast in Sonoma County around Bodega Bay. However, Highway 1 is not fast driving. It's scenic, mostly two-lanes and winding (as it follows the coastal mountains). Plan on some slow driving when taking this route. It's best for those who want a scenic vacation, before heading inland to the wineries.

HIGHWAY 29 (North-South)

Highway 29 is the main north-south highway through Napa County, which means it's also slow going during high traffic times. This highway begins in Vallejo in the south and winds up in Napa Valley. The good news is you'll see dozens upon dozens of wineries along the way and it's your main source of reaching the many other smaller roads that head either east or west to other parts of the valley.

HIGHWAY 12 (East-West)

This state highway runs mostly east-west and is one of the ways you can travel between Napa and Sonoma County. We'll join this highway in Napa, where it will eventually cross over into Sonoma on the southern end, briefly traveling north along Sonoma Valley (and some great wineries) before heading west again after Kenwood. It then continues on past Santa Rosa to Sebastopol.

HIGHWAY 121 (North-South)

Highway 121 is another state highway that travels north along the valley, though it veers east enough to be able to get you from Sonoma to Napa. It begins in southern Sonoma County, then it heads up past many wineries in Sonoma (called Arnold Drive locally), then just before the town of Sonoma, it heads east and makes its way to the city of Napa. Past Napa, it continues on a northeast pattern until it exits the county.

Share your experiences online at wineopolis.com

HIGHWAY 128 (Northwest-Southeast)

This state route can be described in one word: rambling. But luckily, it mostly rambles through the wine country so it's a very handy highway to travel. It enters Napa County from the east, past Lake Berryessa, through St. Helena on up to Calistoga, then travels through west Napa Valley until it heads into Sonoma eventually passing through Alexander Valley (and even more great vineyards). From there it keeps heading northwest until it hits the Pacific Ocean.

HIGHWAY 116 (North-South)

This is another smaller state route that really runs a little northwest-southeast. It's a quieter and less-traveled highway that winds along the Russian River through most of Sonoma County until it spills out into the Pacific Ocean.

Local Transportation Options

Alright, so you made it here. Now what? Don't forget, Napa and Sonoma County are mostly rural, with a city or two in the mix. If you've driven here or rented a car, then you're golden. But, sometimes the thought of *driving* doesn't seem that enticing when you're *wine tasting*. So, we've listed some local transport options so you can leave the driving to someone else while you enjoy your wine.

Limos, Shuttle Buses & Wine Tours

No, we're not in Hollywood. But you wouldn't know it from the number of limousines driving around Napa and Sonoma. Wine is glamorous, so why not have a glamorous vehicle? You'll find a multitude of limo companies when you stay here. What's also popular are the many shuttle bus services that also offer wine tours. A wine tour is when you pay a package fee and then take a private car or board a shuttle bus and visit anywhere from three to five wineries, have a boxed lunch, and then return at the end of the day. It's a good deal for those looking not to drive.

    Note: Most of these companies can service both Napa and Sonoma County (therefore we'll go alphabetically). They also can be as laid back or as involved as you like in customizing your itinerary. Prices are impossible to quote, as they vary depending on car size, number of occupants, number of hours, season, etc. So we'll give you the basics.

Beau Wine Tours & Limo Service

800-387-2328
www.beauwinetours.com

Beau Wine Tours & Limo is like having your own personal concierge set up your wine tasting itinerary for you. All you have to do is ride, relax and taste. They also offer gourmet lunches as well. Tours are available via limo or shuttle van. If you don't want to tour, then you can simply rent their limousine.

California Wine Tours

4075 Solano Avenue, Napa, CA 94558 /
22455 Broadway, Sonoma, CA 95476 / 800-294-6386
www.californiawinetours.com

California Wine Tours is a large scale operation and they can accommodate groups of any size. You can have your pick of cars too, from sedans, limos, vans and mini-buses. They even have a line of hybrid vehicles. There's really nothing they can't offer, so they're worth looking into.

Classic Convertible Wine Tours

707-226-9227
www.antiquetours.net

Why travel by limo when you can travel in a classic 1947 Packard convertible? They specialize in taking customers to small, boutique wineries that are off the beaten path or you can go to mainstream wineries (or a combination). Prices depend on the number of passengers and hours. You can also add a picnic lunch (for an extra fee).

Napa Valley Tours & Transportation

707-251-9463
www.nvtt.net

This transportation company has quite an extensive fleet and can accommodate one person on up to groups of 35 from their range of sedans, limos, suburbans, and mini-coaches. They even have an SUV limo. In addition to their wine tours, they have flat rates to and from the airports in San Francisco and Oakland (ranges from $225 - $285 depending on number of passengers).

Share your experiences online at wineopolis.com

Napa Winery Shuttle

707-257-1950

www.wineshuttle.com

No, they're not a limo service. But they have very comfortable shuttles that will allow you to sip wine all day long and not worry about the road. And, it's cheaper. They only service Napa Valley, but can pick you up at almost any Napa hotel, motel and B&B, and then return you after the tour. A gourmet lunch is served partway through the tour at V. Sattui Winery (that has a great gourmet deli). It makes for a fun day.

Pacific Limousine

877-333-3613

www.pacificlimo.com

Pacific Limo is mostly a limo and car service that will take you almost anywhere you need to go in Napa and Sonoma. Their limos usually run around $55 fee per hour, but they do offer all-day wine tours. You'll have to visit their website for an itinerary. Additionally, they service the airports of San Francisco and Oakland for a flat rate of $180.

Pure Luxury

800-626-5466

www.pureluxury.com

www.pureluxurywinetours.com

Pure Luxury definitely lives up to its name. They have a full range of vehicles to meet just about any need whether it's a private limo, a shuttle van for an all-day wine tour, or a chartered bus. Their tours cover almost every area of Napa and Sonoma Valley. What's really cool is their Eco Wine tour that takes you to all the organic and biodynamic wineries in Sonoma's Dry Creek Valley.

Public Transportation

When we say public transportation, we're talking about the bus. There are some local, inexpensive buses in both Napa and Sonoma. It's a great way to get in-between towns if you don't want to have to switch hotels. Some of the cities have their own bus lines that run routes within the city limits. You'll need to check with each city and see what municipal bus lines they have available.

Share your experiences online at wineopolis.com

The Vine (Formerly Napa Valley Transit)

1151 Pearl Street, Napa, CA 94559 / 800-696-6443
www.nctpa.net/vine.cfm

Once known as the Napa Valley Transit (NVT), The Vine is a municipal bus that services most of Napa Valley starting from Vallejo in the south, up through Calistoga in the north (even through to Santa Rosa in Sonoma). They have daily service, though it is somewhat limited on the weekends so check their website for an up-to-date schedule. They take only exact change and currently the fares range from $1.35-$2.90 for adults.

Sonoma County Transit

335 West Robles Avenue, Santa Rosa, CA 95407 / 800-345-7433
www.sctransit.com

The Sonoma County Transit (SCT) runs from Petaluma in the south up to Cloverdale in the north. It also goes east to Sonoma and west to Occidental. But mainly, it stays on the Highway 101 corridor through the middle of Sonoma County. They have many daily routes, seven days a week. Check their website for hours and fares. Regular fares currently run from $1.25 - $3.45 for adults.

Golden Gate Transit

707-541-2000 / 415-455-2000
www.goldengatetransit.org

The Golden Gate Transit (GGT) makes frequent trips across the North Bay Area, which encompasses San Francisco, up through Marin County, to Santa Rosa in Sonoma County. Cash fares require exact change and currently run from $8.40 - $9.25 for adults when traveling between Sonoma County and San Francisco. The line also hits many other areas in Sonoma besides Santa Rosa, including Petaluma, Sonoma, Rohnert Park, and Sebastopol.

Taxi in Wine Country?

When looking to write a section for taxi cabs, we realized there's not much to say. Unlike the big cities, Napa and Sonoma are small towns so there really aren't any taxi cabs waiting at the curb to take you wherever you need to go. But there are a few places in Napa and Sonoma you can call if you need to use this mode of transportation.

Share your experiences online at wineopolis.com

Napa County: Black Tie Taxi 707-259-1000, Napa Valley Cab (Napa) 707-257-6444, Taxi Cabernet (St. Helena) 707-963-2620

Sonoma County: A-C Taxi (Santa Rosa) 707-526-4888, George's Taxi (Santa Rosa) 707-546-3322 and (Healdsburg) 707-544-4444, Vern's Taxi Service (Sonoma) 707-938-8885

Tasting Wine .... Responsibly

So far, we have talked *a lot* about wine and wine tasting. Just as important is enjoying wine wisely, safely and responsibly. Basically, practice common sense when in Wine Country. Here's a brief refresher worth sharing.

- *Appoint a designated driver or hire a driver.* You never want to drink and drive. And even though you will (maybe) be spitting out most of your wine, you still are ingesting some alcohol. It is best to have a designated driver who is not drinking or for you to make alternate transportation plans.
- *Use the dump buckets.* You will still be able to drink some wine, but if you want to taste four to five wines per winery and visit a few wineries, you will need to spit out your wine. We're here to taste and enjoy, not get tipsy at the first winery.
- *Limit to four wines per tasting.* Most wineries only offer about four wines, but others have many, many flights available and before you know it, you can taste a dozen wines at your first winery. If you're planning on a day of several wineries, it's best to stick to only a few glasses per winery.
- *Don't bring outside alcohol to a winery.* This is just plain rude. If you want to drink and picnic at a winery, then plan on buying a bottle of their wine. If you have a bottle you want to picnic with, then go to a park (there are tons of them around).
- *Make room at the tasting bar for others.* Sometimes Wine Country can get crowded. It is courteous to allow others to stand next to you while at the tasting bar. If the winery is particularly crowded, then step away from the bar with your glass until you are ready for the next pour.
- *Taste whites first.* You'll want to start with the lighter, fruitier wines before you taste the heavier reds. Once you have a red wine, the subtle aromas of a white wine will be lost on you. Basic rule of thumb – follow the recommended tasting order at the winery.
- *Don't wear cologne or perfume.* Body scents will make it impossible for you to smell the wine. So don't ruin that experience for yourself or others.

There, we're done. Some tips and safety reminders so your days of wine tasting are a delight and most enjoyable.

Share your experiences online at wineopolis.com

VI. SOME WINE TERMS YOU NEED TO KNOW

Acidity: refers to the level of tartness in a wine based on the acids present in the grape. These acids help counteract the sugar and balances out the flavor of the wine.

Aftertaste: the flavor that lingers in the mouth after the wine has been swirled around and spit out or swallowed. The aftertaste can be long or short, with a longer time being preferable.

Aerate: occurs when wine is opened and meets the air (either in the bottle or by being poured into a glass). The air helps release the flavor of the wine.

Alcohol: In wine, this refers to ethyl alcohol, which acts like a preservative in wine, thus allowing it to age. It is a by-product of fermentation.

American Viticultural Association (AVA): refers to a geographic region that has unique characteristics in the climate and soil that affect how grapes grow. These regions are officially designated by the Alcohol Tobacco Tax and Trade Bureau and will distinguish where the grapes come from in a wine. (See *appellation*).

Appearance: refers to how a wine looks, usually defined by its color, clarity, and brightness.

Appellation: a specific geographic area where grapes are grown (officially designated as an AVA in the U.S.). For a wine to claim an appellation, 85% or more of the grapes used in that wine must come from that region.

Aroma: in wine terms, it means the scents that are present in a wine, usually directly from the fruit. It can also be used to describe different fruit scents present in a wine (such as currant, apple, and pear). The longer a wine ages, the less fruit-based aroma it will have, giving it a fuller bouquet of smells. (see *bouquet*).

Balance: the harmony of different elements of a wine such as its acidity, sweetness and tannin content.

Barrel: a large container in the shape of a cylinder made from oak that is used to store and age wine. A barrel usually holds up to 240 regular sized wine bottles (750ml).

Blend: a combination of different wines to create a new wine with different complexity and tastes. Blending occurs after the wines have been fermented.

Body: the perceived lightness or heaviness of a wine when tasted in the mouth. Red wines tend to be full-bodied and white wines have a lighter body.

Bordeaux Blend: the mixing together of several grape varietals (known to be grown in the Bordeaux region of France) to make a more complex red or white wine. Includes the following grapes for red: Cabernet Sauvignon, Merlot, Cabernet Franc, Petite Verdot, and Malbec; and for whites includes: Sauvignon Blanc and Sémillon. (See *Meritage*).

Bouquet: the odor and smell of a wine once it has aged. The smell becomes more intense when the wine is swirled in the glass.

Brut: a dry Champagne and/or sparkling white wine.

Cabernet Franc: a grape originally from the Bordeaux region of France that is used for a red wine that is lighter and more subtle than the Cabernet Sauvignon grape.

Cabernet Sauvignon: another grape from Bordeaux used to make very full red wines with high tannins (thus more dry). Grows well in warmer climates.

Cask: a large wooden container that holds wine.

Champagne: a sparkling white wine that is made in the Champagne region of France (thus the name). There is a second fermentation period that occurs in the bottle, giving the wine a high concentration of bubbles.

Chardonnay: a green-skinned grape from several regions in France, used for white wines, as well as Champagne and sparkling wines.

Clarity: a wine with good clarity is lacking in particles and other floating substances when observed in the glass.

Cloudiness: a wine that is cloudy has particles present in the wine that can affect the taste by making it seem murky; usually the mark of a bad or spoiled wine.

Complexity: the different flavors and aromas of a wine that affect the taste as well as the aftertaste.

Cork: bark from a cork tree that is used as a bottle stopper in wine bottles.

Dessert Wine: a sweet wine that is very flavorful, but usually has a lower alcohol content and is best enjoyed with sweet desserts.

Dry: a wine that is low in sugar, having been converted to alcohol, and therefore is not sweet; can also indicate a high level of acidity.

Fermentation: the process by which yeast interacts with sugar and creates alcohol and carbon dioxide, thus making wine from the juice of grapes.

Filtration: the process of running wine through a filter to weed out loose particles. Too much filtration can strip a wine's flavor and aroma.

Finish: the final impression a wine has made after the taste has left the mouth.

Flat: refers to a sparkling wine that has lost its bubbles or a wine that is lacking acidity and thus tastes dull.

Flight: a selection of wines for tasting (usually between 3-8 glasses).

Fortified wine: a wine that has alcohol added to it. Examples include port, sherry and cordials.

Fruity: a wine that has an aroma relating to a fruit, such as pear, apple, cherry, black currant, and raspberry. Mostly present in young wines without much aging.

Fumé Blanc: first coined by Napa Valley winemaker Robert Mondavi to describe a Sauvignon Blanc that is drier. Nowadays refers to a lot of white wines containing either just the Sauvignon Blanc grape or blended with Sémillon.

Gewürztraminer: a light-skinned pinkish grape from Germany that makes a fruity white wine.

Hectare: unit of measurement used in Europe to determine the square measurement of a vineyard. It is estimated to be roughly the size of 2.4 acres.

Initial Taste: the first impression of a wine when it hits the mouth.

Laying Down: the act of laying a wine bottle on its side for aging so that the cork remains wet at all times and does not dry out.

Share your experiences online at wineopolis.com

Legs: the long marks left on the side of a wine glass consisting of wine droplets as a wine is swirled in the glass.

Malbec: a dark-skinned grape also from Bordeaux, France used to make red wines or commonly blended with other wines.

Maturation: the process of aging wine in wood (such as an oak barrel) versus a bottle.

Meritage: an American term describing a red wine that is made from a blend of Bordeaux varietals (both red and white).

Methode Champenoise: the method used in Champagne, France for making sparkling wines that go through a second fermentation in the bottle.

Merlot: A dark-skinned grape native to France that makes a smoother, softer red wine that requires less aging.

Nebbiolo: an Italian grape that is used for a red wine that is very spicy with a hint of tobacco.

Non-Vintage (NV): denotes a wine that is a blend of grapes from different years as well as different vineyards and varietals.

Nose: the overall fragrance of a wine.

Oaky: a wine that has aged too long will cause the flavor of the oak to overpower the flavor of the grape.

Oenology: the study of wine, also called *enology*.

Organic Wine: wines that are produced without any added sulfur products.

Oxidized: this occurs when a wine has had too much exposure to air; causes the wine to lose some of its flavor and freshness.

Palate: refers to the upper region of the mouth and helps determine the effect of a wine as far as taste and feel.

Pasteurization: the process of flash heating a wine to kill off bacteria.

Petite Sirah: a grape that originated in France, but is mostly grown in California. The grape is called Durif, after botanist Francois Durif, and makes a red wine that is spicy and high in tannins.

Petit Verdot: another dark-skinned grape from the Bordeaux region that is mostly used in red wine blends, but when used alone makes a very full-bodied red wine.

PH: measurement of the acidity of a wine. The lower the PH, the higher the acidity.

Pinot Noir: a very dark-skinned French grape that creates a complex and rich red wine. It is one of the most difficult grapes to cultivate and process into wine. It is most often grown in the French Burgundy regions and in other cooler climates.

Port: a sweet wine that is fortified with alcohol, named after the Douro Valley region in Portugal.

Reserve: an amount of wine set aside by the winemaker to be aged longer or produced to a superior quality and is typically offered in more limited production.

Residual Sugar: the sugar content that is left in a wine after fermentation.

Share your experiences online at wineopolis.com

Riesling: often referred to as a Johannisberg Riesling, it is a light-skinned grape native to Germany that produces a sweet white wine.

Rosé: a pink tinted wine that is made when the skin of a dark-skinned grape is left on long enough during processing to give the wine a hint of color.

Sangiovese: a red grape from the Chianti region in Italy used to make a light-bodied to medium-bodied red wine.

Sauvignon Blanc: a green-skinned grape from the French Bordeaux region that makes a crisp and dry white wine.

Sémillon: another green-skinned grape from Bordeaux that creates a much sweeter wine and is often blended with a Sauvignon Blanc.

Sommelier: a person who is trained and knowledgeable in the selection and servicing of wine; usually a person in a restaurant.

Sparkling Wine: a wine that is bubbly due to the non-release of carbon dioxide, a by-product of fermentation. The first sparkling wines were made in Champagne, France and only ones produced in that region can be officially called Champagne. When made elsewhere, they are called sparkling wines. Usually made from Chardonnay or Pinot Noir grapes.

Still Wine: refers to a wine that is not bubbly.

Syrah: a grape from the Rhône region in France that is used to make red wine that is full-bodied and requires more aging than other reds.

Tannins: a compound that is found naturally in grape skins seeds and stems, as well as oak barrels that causes a wine to taste more tart. Older reds that have aged longer have less tannin than younger ones and are therefore less sharp.

Tasting: the act of sipping a wine to determine its qualities by using the senses of sight, texture, smell and taste.

Terroir: a French word that is used to describe all the geographic and climate factors affecting grapes such as the soil, temperature, topography of the land, amount of moisture and amount of sunlight.

Varietal: a type of grape; also a wine that is named after the variety of grape used to produce the wine.

Vat: a large open container where wine is fermented and blended; can be made of wood, stainless steel or concrete.

Vinification: the process of making wine from grapes.

Vintage: when on a bottle, it refers to the year the grapes were harvested.

Viognier: a light-skinned grape from the Rhône region in France that produces a fruity and complex white wine.

Woody: similar to the term oaky, it refers to wines that have aged for too long in an oak barrel and have taken on the flavor and aroma of the wood.

Yeast: a single-celled fungi that is added to grapes to aid in converting the sugar to alcohol and releasing carbon dioxide, thus fermenting the wine.

Zinfandel: a red grape whose origins are debated, but most agree stems from Croatia. It is a popular variety in California and makes a well-balanced, robust red wine. The grape has a high sugar content, which when fermented can give the wine an alcohol content higher than other wines.

Share your experiences online at wineopolis.com

INDEX

A

Ad Hoc, 54, 55
Alexander Valley, 28, 95, 96, 116, 121, 122, 123, 146, 172
All Seasons Café, 59
American Indian Trading Company, 70
American Vintage, 98
American Viticultural Area, 3
Anderson's Conn Valley, 16, 36
Angèle, 53
Aromas, 11, 48, 49, 50, 51, 124, 125, 126, 127
Arrowood Vineyards, 106
Asian, 53, 54, 84, 154
Atlas Peak, 19
Autumn, 6, 78
AVA, 3, 19, 20, 21, 35, 96, 97, 98, 177

B

B&B, 18, 77, 78, 79, 80, 84, 86, 87, 88, 89, 155, 156, 158, 159, 160, 161, 162, 163, 174
bakery, 57, 67
balloon rides, 64
BBQ, 54, 55
Beaulieu Vineyard, 34
bed & breakfast, 7, 18, 76, 79, 82, 84, 106, 152, 155, 157, 159
Bella Vineyards, 120
Bennett Lane Winery, 33, 47
Bennett Valley, 92, 96, 112
Black Stallion, 16, 23
Bodega Bay, 3, 95, 171
Bordeaux, 24, 36, 41, 44, 80, 97, 102, 104, 121, 177, 178, 179, 180
Bottle Shock, 46
Brut, 22, 32, 100, 105, 177
Budget, 5

C

Cabernet Franc, 19, 29, 30, 32, 35, 38, 108, 111, 177, 178
Cabernet Sauvignon, 13, 19, 20, 21, 23, 24, 25, 26, 28, 29, 30, 31, 32, 33, 34, 35, 36, 37, 38, 39, 40, 41, 42, 43, 44, 45, 46, 47, 58, 96, 97, 98, 100, 101, 104, 107, 108, 109, 110, 111, 112, 113, 116, 117, 118, 119, 120, 122, 123, 144, 177, 178
Café La Haye, 128
Cakebread Cellars, 31, 34
Calistoga, 18, 19, 27, 33, 44, 45, 46, 47, 58, 59, 69, 70, 71, 77, 83, 84, 172, 175
Calistoga Pottery, 70
Carneros, 20, 22, 25, 92, 97, 99, 100, 102, 105, 107, 115, 117
CASK 23 S.L.V., 24
caves, 37, 47, 100, 105, 116, 120
Ca'Toga Galleria D'Arte, 70
Celadon, 52
Chalk Hill, 92, 96, 116, 118
Charbono, 46
Chardonnay, 3, 10, 13, 19, 20, 21, 22, 23, 24, 25, 28, 31, 32, 33, 34, 35, 36, 38, 39, 40, 41, 42, 43, 45, 46, 96, 97, 98, 100, 103, 105, 106, 107, 108, 109, 110, 112, 113, 114, 116, 117, 118, 120, 121, 122, 123, 178, 180
Charles Creek Vineyard, 100
Charles Krug, 4
Chateau Montelena, 34, 46
Chateau St. Jean, 92, 108, 111
cheeses, 13, 26, 41, 65, 67, 68, 109, 112, 113, 123, 134, 142
Chiles Valley, 19
Chinese, 46, 47, 82
chocolate, 27, 69, 82, 105, 131, 133, 135, 144
Cinsault, 106
Cline Cellars, 99, 115, 117, 141
Clos Du Bois, 121
Clos Du Val, 16, 24, 39
Cloverdale, 2, 95, 122, 123, 135, 159, 171, 175
coffee, 2, 59, 70, 82, 94, 143, 145, 155
Cole's Chop House, 52
Conn Creek, 16, 36
Count Agoston Haraszthy, 4
Culinary Institute of America, 57
Cuvée, 53, 105

181

D

Darioush, 23, 41
Dean & Deluca, 67
Diamond Mountain, 19
Domaine Chandon, 26, 55
Dry Creek Valley, 95, 96, 97, 119, 120, 121, 122, 123, 157, 174
Dryness, 11
dump bucket, 10, 12, 176

E

Elévage, 24
excursion, 5, 28, 64, 91, 145, 165
Étoile, 28, 55

F

Failla, 16, 42
Finish, 11, 48, 49, 50, 51, 124, 125, 126, 127, 178
Flavors, 11, 13, 48, 49, 50, 51, 124, 125, 126, 127
Flavors of the Region, 13
Flight, 10, 178
Francis Ford Coppola, 2, 29, 32
Frank Family Vineyards, 44
Frank Gehry, 38
Fruity wines, 12
Full bodied wines, 13
Fumé Blanc, 24, 30, 37, 119, 178

G

Gary Farrell Winery, 120
General's Daughter, 129
George Yount, 4, 18
Gewürztraminer, 106, 178
Geyserville, 28, 93, 95, 121, 122, 147, 158
Glen Ellen, 96, 104, 106, 130, 143, 144, 154
Gloria Ferrer, 92, 100
Gold Rush, 3
Goosecross Cellars, 28
Gottlieb Groezinger, 4
gourmet, 13, 41, 52, 54, 65, 67, 69, 79, 84, 109, 110, 112, 113, 118, 123, 128, 129, 146, 156, 157, 173, 174
Grape Rush, 4
Green Valley, 97, 114
Grgich, 16, 34
Gustave Niebaum, 32

H

Hall Winery, 36
Hartwell Vineyards, 26
Healdsburg, 27, 94, 95, 116, 118, 119, 120, 133, 134, 141, 145, 146, 156, 157, 171, 176
Heitz Wine Cellars, 40
HESS, 43
Highway 1, 2, 33, 47, 93, 94, 95, 96, 99, 100, 101, 105, 106, 108, 109, 111, 115, 117, 123, 131, 135, 140, 141, 145, 146, 147, 154, 171, 175
Highway 101, 2, 93, 94, 95, 96, 131, 140, 175
HIGHWAY 116, 172
Highway 12, 33, 47, 94, 96, 99, 100, 101, 105, 106, 108, 109, 111, 115, 117, 123, 131, 140, 141, 145, 146, 147, 154, 171
HIGHWAY 121, 171
HIGHWAY 128, 172
Highway 29, 17, 18, 30, 37, 68, 69, 79, 171
hotel, 7, 18, 54, 58, 64, 76, 77, 78, 79, 80, 82, 83, 95, 109, 119, 130, 152, 153, 154, 155, 156, 158, 168, 169, 174
Howell Mountain, 19

I

Imagery Estate Winery, 106
Inglenook, 29, 32
Iron Horse Vineyards, 114
Italian, 26, 40, 53, 70, 100, 117, 119, 130, 153, 179

J

Jacob Schram, 47
Jacuzzi, 81, 84, 86, 87, 88, 89, 92, 99, 100, 115, 117, 140, 154, 158, 160, 161, 162, 163
jazz, 58, 65

Joseph Phelps Vineyard, 44
Judgment of Paris, 26, 39, 46

K

Kaz Winery, 110
Kendall-Jackson, 92, 96, 114
Kenwood, 92, 96, 101, 103, 106, 108, 110, 111, 112, 131, 154, 171
KENWOOD VINEYARDS, 101
Knight's Valley, 97
Kuleto Estate, 16, 40

L

La Toque, 54
Lancaster Estate Winery, 116
Landmark Vineyards, 103, 108
LEDSON WINERY, 109
Lincoln Theater, 66
live music, 65
Local Transportation, 172
Louis M. Martini Winery, 42
Lynmar Estate, 92, 112

M

Malbec, 35, 106, 108, 111, 177, 179
Mario Andretti, 2
Marsanne, 108, 115
Martinelli Winery, 116
Martini House, 58
Matanzas Creek Winery, 112
Mayacamas, 17, 93, 97
Meat & Seafood, 14
Mediterranean, 6, 14, 36, 39, 52, 56, 79, 110, 111
Mendocino, 95, 123
Merlot, 10, 13, 19, 20, 21, 23, 24, 25, 26, 27, 29, 32, 33, 35, 38, 39, 45, 47, 96, 101, 107, 108, 109, 112, 113, 117, 118, 121, 177, 179
Mexican, 53
Moet-Hennessey, 26
Moroccan, 52
motel, 76, 81, 152, 157, 174
Mount Veeder, 20, 43
Mourvèdre, 106, 115
Mumm, 16, 32
Muscat, 23, 33, 106, 116, 117
museum, 22, 43, 66, 67, 69, 70, 71, 101, 115, 117, 141, 143, 144
Mustards, 55, 57

N

Napa County, 2, 17, 19, 65, 93, 169, 171, 172, 176
Napa Symphony, 66
Napa Valley, 2, 3, 17, 18, 19, 22, 23, 24, 25, 26, 27, 28, 29, 30, 31, 32, 33, 34, 35, 36, 37, 39, 40, 41, 42, 43, 44, 45, 46, 47, 57, 64, 65, 66, 68, 69, 76, 79, 80, 96, 171, 172, 173, 174, 175, 176, 178

Nebbiolo, 100, 117, 179
North Coast, 20, 96, 97
Northern California Wine Country, 1, 2, 3, 4, 5, 6, 7, 10, 12, 14, 18, 20, 22, 24, 26, 28, 30, 32, 34, 36, 38, 40, 42, 44, 46, 48, 50, 52, 54, 56, 58, 60, 62, 64, 66, 68, 70, 72, 74, 76, 78, 80, 82, 84, 86, 88, 94, 96, 98, 100, 102, 104, 106, 108, 110, 112, 114, 116, 118, 120, 122, 124, 126, 128, 130, 132, 134, 136, 138, 140, 142, 144, 146, 148, 150, 152, 154, 156, 158, 160, 162, 167, 168, 170, 172, 174, 176, 178, 180

O

Oak Knoll, 16, 20, 23, 35, 41
Oakiness, 11
Oakville, 16, 19, 20, 28, 30, 37
olive oil, 14, 68, 117, 129, 140
Olives, 14
opera, 34, 35, 43, 47, 58, 65, 118, 142, 144, 169, 173
Opus One, 16, 30
Oxbow Public Market, 65

P

Pacific Ocean, 2, 6, 14, 20, 93, 95, 97, 172
park, 18, 22, 28, 32, 38, 44, 45, 47, 48, 49, 50, 51, 64, 68, 69, 79, 81, 100, 105, 107, 114, 124, 125, 126, 127, 131, 142, 143, 144, 145, 176, 177, 178, 179, 180
Peju, 16, 30
Pendleton Estate Vineyards, 92, 123
Petit Verdot, 24, 35, 179
Petite Sirah, 19, 42, 102, 119, 123, 179
petrified forest, 71
picnic, 24, 37, 38, 39, 45, 47, 57, 66, 67, 69, 99, 103, 108, 109, 110, 111, 112, 115, 119, 121, 141, 143, 173, 176
Pinot Noir, 10, 20, 22, 24, 27, 31, 32, 34, 35, 36, 38, 39, 42, 45, 97, 100, 101, 102, 103, 104, 105, 107, 110, 114, 118, 120, 121, 123, 133, 179, 180
private tour, 26
prix fixe, 54
Public Transportation, 174

Q

QUIVIRA VINEYARDS, 119,

R

Ramey Wine Cellars, 118
Ravenswood Winery, 102
Raymond Burr Vineyards, 120
resort, 18, 56, 69, 76, 83, 152, 155, 169
Restaurants, 52, 78, 128
Riesling, 13, 23, 35, 46, 112, 180
Robert Mondavi, 30, 37, 65, 178
Rockpile, 97
Rodney Strong Vineyards, 119
Rohnert Park, 95, 131, 169, 175
Rombauer, 25, 44
Rosé, 22, 38, 100, 105, 113, 118, 180
Roussane, 108
Rubicon, 29, 32
Russian River Valley, 27, 95, 96, 97, 112, 116, 118, 120, 135, 158
Rutherford, 16, 19, 20, 29, 30, 31, 32, 34, 36, 38, 56, 81

S

sake, 56
San Francisco, 2, 3, 13, 93, 94, 95, 101, 107, 123, 128, 168, 169, 171, 173, 174, 175
Sangiovese, 21, 100, 117, 119, 180
Santa Rosa, 2, 93, 94, 96, 109, 110, 112, 113, 114, 131, 132, 144, 145, 155, 156, 168, 169, 170, 171, 175, 176
Sauvignon Blanc, 12, 13, 20, 21, 22, 26, 27, 33, 34, 37, 38, 45, 96, 97, 107, 108, 116, 118, 119, 121, 177, 178, 180
Sbragia Family Vineyards, 122
Schramsberg, 16, 47
Schug, 92, 102, 107
seasons, 6, 59, 82
Sebastopol, 96, 112, 114, 158, 171, 175
Selby Winery, 92, 118
shops, 2, 13, 64, 65, 78, 80, 82, 84, 94, 95, 100, 140, 141, 144, 147, 152, 153, 155, 158
Shuttle Bus, 172
Siduri Wines, 92, 110
Silver Oak, 28
Silverado Trail, 17, 18, 23, 24, 25, 26, 27, 32, 36, 39, 41, 42, 44, 79, 82
Silverado Vineyards, 26
Smoked foods, 13
Sonoma Coast, 97

Sonoma County, 2, 27, 93, 94, 95, 96, 97, 98, 99, 103, 123, 140, 145, 154, 159, 168, 169, 170, 171, 172, 175, 176
Sonoma Valley, 97, 98, 101, 102, 103, 104, 106, 108, 109, 110, 111, 112, 113, 121, 143, 153, 154, 171, 174
Soscol Avenue, 2, 18, 53, 77
sparkling, 22, 28, 32, 38, 44, 45, 47, 64, 100, 105, 107, 114, 144, 177, 178, 179, 180
Spicy foods, 13
spitting, 10, 176
Spring, 6, 20, 38, 44, 58, 78, 92, 133
St. Francis, 92, 110, 112, 113
St. Helena, 18, 21, 25, 29, 30, 31, 32, 34, 36, 38, 40, 42, 44, 55, 56, 57, 58, 64, 67, 68, 69, 81, 82, 92, 97, 119, 172, 176
Stag's Leap, 24, 26, 39
Sterling Vineyards, 45
sub-appellations, 19
Summer, 6, 16, 38, 42, 46, 133
Summers Estate, 46
sushi, 56, 131
Sutter Home, 16, 40
Sweet wines, 12
Swiss Hotel, 94, 130
Syrah, 19, 31, 33, 42, 47, 79, 97, 102, 103, 104, 110, 118, 120, 180

T

Tannins, 10, 11, 180
tasting, 3, 4, 5, 7, 9, 10, 11, 12, 13, 14, 21, 22, 23, 25, 27, 28, 29, 30, 31, 32, 33, 34, 35, 36, 37, 38, 39, 40, 41, 42, 43, 44, 45, 46, 47, 55, 64, 66, 76, 79, 91, 94, 95, 99, 100, 101, 102, 103, 104, 105, 106, 107, 108, 109, 110, 111, 112, 114, 115, 116, 117, 118, 119, 120, 121, 122, 123, 129, 130, 132, 133, 134, 140, 141, 142, 143, 144, 146, 154, 159, 165, 172, 173, 176, 178
Taxi, 175, 176
terroir, 20, 43, 98, 105, 106
Textures, 11
The Girl & The Fig, 129, 153
The Red Grape, 129
theater, 65, 66
Traveling by Air, 168
Traveling by Auto, 170
Traveling by Train or Bus, 169

TREFETHEN, 35
Trincheros, 40
TWOMEY CELLARS, 27

U
US HIGHWAY 101, 170

V
V.Sattui Winery, 38
Valley of the Moon, 98, 108
Varietal, 10, 33, 48, 49, 50, 51, 124, 125, 126, 127, 180
Viognier, 20, 35, 41, 123, 180
viticulture, 4

W
Wattle Creek Winery, 122
White Burgundy, 106
White wines, 13
Wild Horse Valley, 21

Windsor, 96, 116, 133
Wine & Food Pairing, 12
wine clubs, 14
Wine Spectator Restaurant, 67
Wine Tasting, 9, 11, 13, 15
Wine Terms, 9, 10, 179
Wine Tour, 172, 173
Winter, 7, 38, 42, 133, 144

Y
Yountville, 16, 18, 20, 21, 26, 28, 54, 55, 66, 80

Z
ZAZU RESTAURANT, 132
ZD Wines, 32
ZIN, 113, 134,
Zinfandel, 19, 20, 21, 25, 31, 38, 40
Zinfandel, 16, 19, 20, 21, 22, 25, 31, 38, 40, 46, 82, 96, 97, 98, 99, 101, 102, 104, 108, 109, 113, 115, 116, 119, 120, 122, 123, 134, 135, 144, 180

Made in the USA
Lexington, KY
10 December 2010